Antifascistas

British and Irish Volunteers in the Spanish Civil War
in Words and Pictures

RICHARD BAXELL ANGELA JACKSON JIM JUMP

Lawrence & Wishart
in association with the
International Brigade Memorial Trust

Antifascistas
was written, compiled and edited
by the authors, with creative advice from
Mick Jones and support and encouragement
from Duncan Longstaff and Marlene Sidaway.
The accompanying exhibition
was designed by Doug Pouch.

Lawrence & Wishart Limited
99a Wallis Road
London E9 5LN

International Brigade Memorial Trust
37 Reginald Road
London E7 9HS

In collaboration with the Cañada Blanch Centre
for Contemporary Spanish Studies

First published 2010

All images are from the collections of the
IBMT or the authors, except where indicated.
Every effort has been made to seek permission
and acknowledge the source of each image.
Where this has proved impossible, we would
welcome further information so that proper
acknowledgement can be given in any
further edition.

British Library Cataloguing in Publication Data.
A catalogue record for this book is available
from the British Library
ISBN 9781 907103 179

Text setting and design Andrew Corbett
Printed and bound by
Butler Tanner & Dennis, Frome

Richard Baxell is the author of *British Volunteers in the Spanish Civil War: The British Battalion in the International Brigades, 1936-1939* (2004, updated in 2007). He studied history as an undergraduate at Middlesex University, before taking an MA at the Institute of Historical Research and a PhD at the London School of Economics and Political Science. A trustee of the International Brigade Memorial Trust, he is currently writing a book on British anti-fascist fighters from 1932 to 1945.

Angela Jackson is the author of *British Women and the Spanish Civil War*, a doctoral thesis first published in 2002 and updated in 2009 for a paperback edition. She lives in Catalonia, where much of her research has focused on the interactions between International Brigaders and local people. Her books include *Beyond the Battlefield: Testimony, Memory and Remembrance of a Cave Hospital in the Spanish Civil War* (2005), a novel, *Warm Earth* (2007) and *At the Margins of Mayhem: Prologue and Epilogue to the Last Great Battle of the Spanish Civil War* (2008). As president of the association No Jubilem La Memòria, she works to promote research and education on the subject of the civil war in the Priorat region of Catalonia.

Jim Jump edited *Poems from Spain: British and Irish International Brigaders on the Spanish Civil War* (2006) and co-edited a Spanish anthology of poems by International Brigaders from the British Isles, *Hablando de leyendas: Poemas para España* (2009). He also edited a bilingual collection of poems by his father, James R Jump, *Poems of War and Peace / Poemas de guerra y de paz* (2007). The son of a British International Brigader and a Spanish Republican refugee, he is a London-based freelance journalist and is an IBMT trustee and editor of its newsletter.

Contents

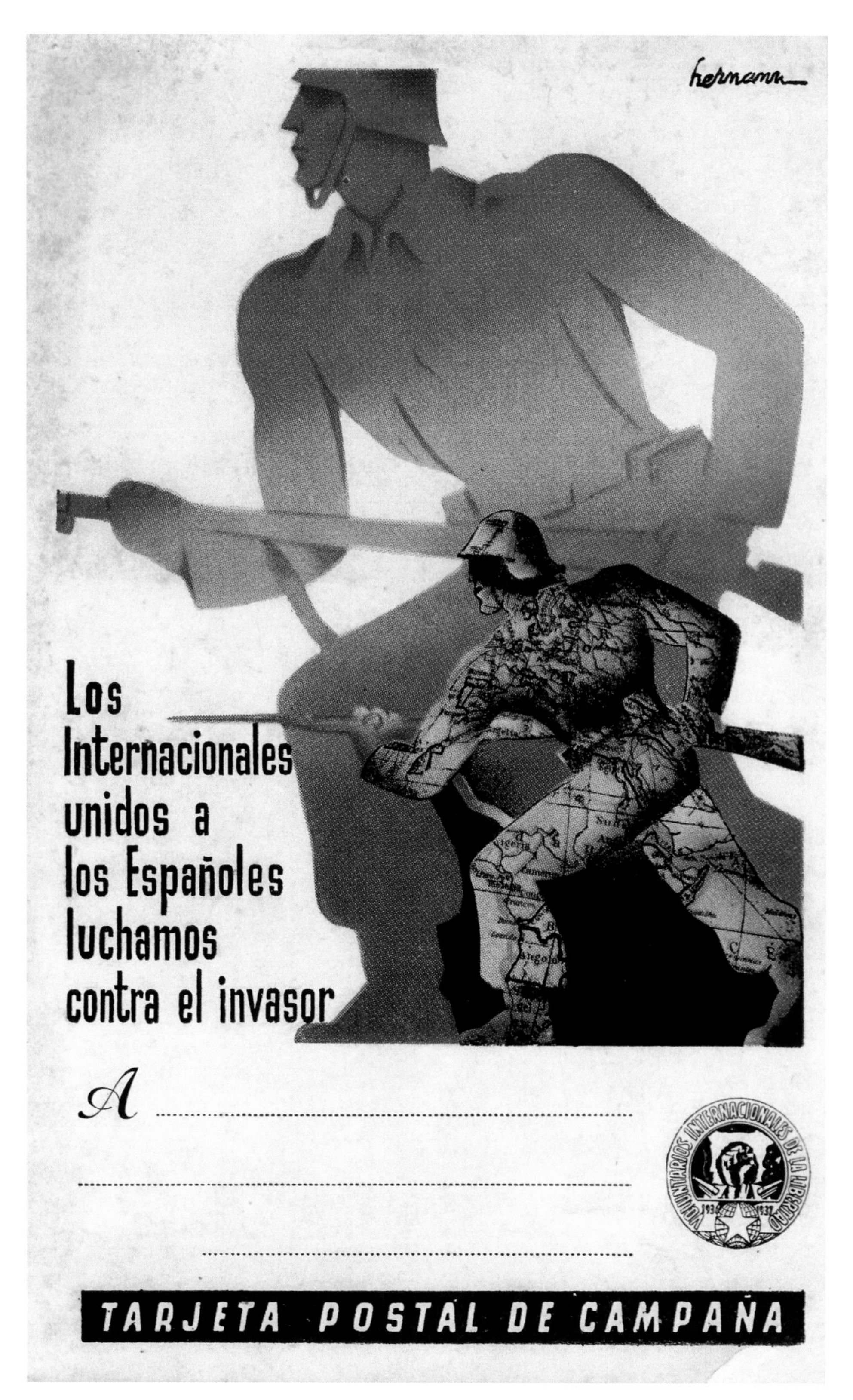

This 1937 postcard says: "We, the Internationals, united with the Spanish, fight against the invader."

Introduction

Paul Preston

THE YEARS FROM 1918 TO 1939 were an era of virtually uninterrupted rightist assault on the organised working class. The crushing of revolution in Germany and Hungary after the First World War was followed by the destruction of the Italian left by Mussolini, the establishment of dictatorships in Spain and Portugal and the defeat of the general strike in Britain. The rise of Hitler saw the annihilation of the most powerful working class movement in Western Europe and in 1934 the Austrian left was smashed by Dollfuss. Austria stands out because there, for the first time, workers took up arms against fascism in 1934. Tragically, it was too late and the domino effect continued in country after country in central Europe.

The Spanish Civil War which broke out in July 1936 was to be the fiercest battle in a European civil war which had been under way since the bolshevik triumph of 1917. The Spanish war was essentially Spanish in origin. In the first two years of the Second Republic in Spain, between 1931 and 1933, a coalition of moderate socialists and middle class liberal Republicans had attempted to carry through a programme of social reform, especially in the countryside. The success of right-wing resistance impelled the socialists to fight the November 1933 elections alone in the hope of establishing an exclusively socialist government. In a system which favoured coalitions, this handed victory to a rightist coalition. Throughout 1934, that coalition overturned the minimal social and religious reforms of 1931–1933. Fearful that the right planned to establish a fascist state, socialists, anarchists and communists rose up in the mining districts of Asturias only to be defeated by the army under the supervision of General Francisco Franco. It was the first battle of the civil war. The right took its revenge in a savage repression which impelled the left to reunite in the Popular Front. In the February 1936 elections, the Popular Front won a narrow victory and immediately began to revive the reforming programme of 1931.

Alarmed by the confidence of the left, the right prepared for war. A military conspiracy was led by General Emilio Mola. The growing fascist party, Falange Española, used terror squads to create the disorder to justify the imposition of an authoritarian regime. The left's response contributed to the spiral of violence. The plotters rose on 18 July not expecting a long war. The rising succeeded in the provincial capitals of conservative Catholic Castile, but was defeated by the workers in Madrid, Barcelona and the major industrial cities of the north. However, once the rebels' strongest card, the brutal colonial Army of Africa, under General Franco, had crossed the Strait of Gibraltar in transport aircraft supplied by Hitler and Mussolini, the over-optimistic coup was converted into a long and bloody civil war.

A militiaman in Barcelona in July 1936 says farewell to his family before leaving for the front.

MARX MEMORIAL LIBRARY

The assistance given to Franco by Hitler and Mussolini was not disinterested, for they knew that, in giving it, they were also undermining the position of the Western powers who covertly applauded the destruction of a Republic they assumed to be a Soviet puppet. It was hardly surprising that the activities of foreign powers would dictate both the course and the outcome of the Spanish Civil War. Much of the energy of the right in Europe during the interwar period was devoted to trying both internationally and domestically to build barriers against both real and perceived revolutionary threats. Fear and suspicion of the Soviet Union had been a major determinant of the diplomacy of the Western powers throughout the 1920s. In the context of world depression and increased working class militancy, anti-bolshevism became even more decisive in the 1930s. The relative tolerance shown initially by Britain and the

United States to both Hitler and Mussolini implied a tacit approval of fascist policies towards the left in general and towards communism in particular.

Accordingly, the war between the Spanish left and right had wide international ramifications. The Spanish Popular Front government turned immediately for help to its French counterpart. Out of fascist solidarity and out of a desire to weaken France, the German and Italian dictators agreed to send aircraft without which the Spanish rebels would not have been able to transport their best troops for use on the Spanish mainland. Similarly, Soviet arms would play a crucial part in the defence of Madrid, not so much out of ideological solidarity but because Stalin did not want to see the French counterweight to Germany weakened.

For Italian, German and Austrian refugees from fascism and Nazism, however, the Spanish Civil War was the first real chance to fight back and eventually to go home. Volunteers from the democracies made the hazardous journey to Spain out of anxiety about what defeat for the Spanish Republic might mean for the rest of the world. The volunteers overcame enormous difficulties to fight for the Republic. Some were out-of-work, others were intellectuals, a few adventurers, but all had come to fight fascism. The International Brigades were organised under the auspices of the Comintern in the late summer and early autumn of 1936 although it is clear that the communists were merely providing channels for a widespread spontaneous movement.

Volunteers from all over the world arrived in Spain via Paris in October and were trained at Albacete. The first units reached Madrid on 8 November and consisted of German and Italian anti-fascists, plus some British, French and Polish left-wingers. Some of them had either fought in the First World War or else had some experience of military service. Accordingly, they were able to pass on much basic military know-how to the Spanish militiamen with whom they fought. Sprinkled among the Spanish defenders at the rate of one to four, the Brigaders both boosted their morale and trained them in the use of machine-guns, in the conservation of ammunition and how to use cover.

Antifascistas

After their crucial role in the defence of Madrid against the initial rebel assault, in December and January the International Brigades played a decisive part in fighting off the various efforts made by the Nationalists to cut the Madrid–La Coruña road to the north west. Casualties among the International Brigades were particularly high. This was hardly surprising, given that they were often used as shock troops and the huge disparity in training and equipment enjoyed by Franco's hardened colonial army. Having failed to capture Madrid in November, after the fall of Málaga in February the rebels renewed their efforts with an attempt to close the circle around the capital. They launched a huge attack through the Jarama valley on the Madrid– Valencia highway to the east of the capital. This was defended fiercely by Republican troops reinforced by the International Brigades. In the view of Hemingway, the attack was "stupidly conceived and insanely executed". The Nationalist front advanced a few miles, but made no strategic gain. Precise estimates vary considerably. It is reasonable to conclude that the Republicans lost a minimum of 10,000 casualties, including some of the best British and American members of the Brigades. Rebel casualties were at the very least 6,000. The International Brigades bore the brunt of the fighting.

Bombs being attached to planes of Hitler's Condor Legion in Spain.

MARX MEMORIAL LIBRA

In March, the Nationalists made further efforts to encircle Madrid by attacking Guadalajara, forty miles north-east of the capital. An army of 50,000, the best-equipped and most heavily armed force yet seen in the war, broke through, but were defeated by a Republican counter-attack involving the Garibaldi Battalion of the International Brigades. Thereafter, as the Republic progressed in the organisation of its Ejército Popular [Popular Army] and as the conflict turned into a more conventional war of large-scale manoeuvre, the Brigades played an important but less central role. After each engagement, there were fewer survivors. Yet after each engagement, they went willingly back into battle. Poorly clad, shod and equipped, they fought on, held together by shared ideals rather than by conventional structures of hierarchy and discipline.

The Brigades played a substantial role in later offensives – the capture of Belchite and Teruel, and also in the final defensive phase of the war following Franco's great offensive through the

spring and summer of 1938. This followed on from the defeat of the Republican attack against Teruel, which briefly held the town from 8 January to 21 February 1938. Within two weeks, the Nationalists launched a gigantic offensive through Aragon and Castellón towards the sea. With 100,000 troops, well covered by 200 tanks and over 600 German and Italian aircraft, they began their advance on 7 March 1938. By 15 April, they had reached the Mediterranean. In July, Franco launched a major attack on Valencia. The Republican forces, including the International Brigades, demonstrated heroic determination in defence and delayed the inexorable Nationalist advance. In late July 1938, to relieve the threat against Valencia, the Republic mounted a spectacular diversion in the form of an attempt to restore contact with Catalonia by an assault across the River Ebro. In the most hard-fought battle of the entire war, the Republican army of 80,000 men crossed the river and broke through the Nationalist lines, although at great cost to the International Brigades. By 1 August, they had reached Gandesa, but Francoist reinforcements were rushed in and the Republicans were subjected to three months of fierce artillery bombardment and sweltering heat. Determined to smash the Republican army, Franco gathered over 30,000 fresh troops with new German equipment. By mid-November, at horrendous cost in casualties, the Francoists had pushed the Republicans out of the territory captured in July. In the hope of changing the attitude of the Western powers, the Republican government decided unilaterally to withdraw its foreign volunteers. A farewell parade was held in Barcelona for the International Brigades on 28 October 1938.

It is difficult to calculate exactly the total number of volunteers. Recent research has reduced earlier estimates of 60,000 to close to 35,000. They had come from fifty different countries to fight against fascism in Spain, most from France, with approximately 2,500 from Great Britain and its empire. In the course of the war, nearly 20 per cent of the international volunteers died and most suffered wounds of varying degrees of severity. In October 1938, more than 12,000 were still in Spain. Those who were not captives in Franco's prisons and concentration camps began the slow journey home or back into exile, often to fates more appalling than anything they had yet suffered. Those who survived were not to return to Spain until after the death of Franco thirty-seven years later.

It is impossible to evaluate with certainty the impact of the International Brigades. On innumerable occasions, at the siege of Madrid, the battles of Jarama, Guadalajara and Brunete, they contributed decisively to Republican survival. Some have argued that a Republican victory would have permitted Hitler's troops to have rolled onto Gibraltar after the defeat of France. But that is the worst kind of counter-factual history. Franco believed, rightly, that he had done Hitler an enormous service in defeating the Republic because of the way in which he had both exposed the weakness of appeasement and specifically altered the balance of power against the Western allies both internationally and also in terms of internal French politics. The Republican victory for which the Brigaders fought might very well have stiffened French resistance, might have avoided the Hitler-Stalin pact, severely dented Mussolini's confidence, and moreover possibly even have avoided the Second World War altogether. However, that is mere speculation. What is certain is that the Spanish Republic severely weakened the military capacity of fascist Italy. Moreover, as long as the Republic fought on, Hitler was unlikely to attack France and therefore the British had longer to rearm.

International Brigaders on a campaign tour following their return to Britain.

MARX MEMORIAL LIBRA

In moral terms, the value of the Brigades as a beacon of anti-fascism was incalculable. On 22 June 1937, shortly before his death in battle, an American volunteer named Gene Wolman wrote to his family as follows: "For the first time in history, for the first time since Fascism began systematically throttling and rending all we hold dear, we are getting the opportunity to fight back. Mussolini rode unopposed... to Rome. Hitler boasts that he took power without bloodshed... In little Asturias the miners made a brave, but unsuccessful stand against the combined reactionaries of Spain. In Ethiopia the Fascist machine was again able to work its will without any unified opposition. Even in Democratic America the majority have had to undergo every sort of oppression without being able to fight back... Here finally the oppressed of the Earth are united, here finally we have weapons, here we can fight back. Here, even if we lose... in the

fight itself, in the weakening of Fascism, we will have won."

Franco's dictatorship was to become the institutionalisation of his victory. He had deliberately fought a slow war of attrition, with horrific purges in each piece of captured territory, as an investment in terror to underpin his future regime. By 31 March 1939, all of Spain was in Nationalist hands. About 350,000 people were killed in the course of the war. At least 50,000 people were shot by the Francoists between 1939 and 1943. Prisoners numbered nearly one million and some were forced into "work battalions" to be used as cheap labour in the construction of dams, bridges, and irrigation canals. The most infamous fruit of their labour was Franco's great mausoleum for the Nationalist war dead, the Valle de los Caídos near El Escorial. About 400,000 went into exile, most never to return. The emotional cost of exile for all of them was incalculable. Most also suffered considerable material privation. Only a small minority who had funds or skills secured a decent living, most often in Latin America. Others nearer Spain usually found themselves forced into the French Foreign Legion, German labour brigades or concentration camps. The need to learn new languages and find work in a hostile environment meant that most exiles had little time to devote to Spain. For those who stayed behind, fear was made a way of life. The population was demoralised. In town and country, informers abounded. Curfews and a system of safe-conducts were in force. Between 1939 and 1944, the so-called Ministry of Justice admitted to a figure of over 190,000 executed or having died in prison. Many released from jail were seriously ill or else demoralised by the fear of being arrested again. Hunger and the virtual impossibility of getting work diminished the combative capacity of the Republicans. Conditions in working class districts were appalling: people in rags searched for scraps, many lived in caves, there were no medical services.

In 1964, General Franco and his supporters were delighted by a noisy year-long celebration of the "Twenty-Five Years of Peace" since the end of the civil war. It began with a solemn Te Deum in the basilica at the Valle de los Caídos. The mass celebrated not peace but victory. Every town and village in Spain was bedecked with posters asserting that the Nationalist war effort had been a religious crusade to purge Spain of the atheistic hordes of the left. For the Caudillo, the defeated were the "canalla [scum] of the Jewish-masonic-communist conspiracy" and the civil war "the struggle of the Patria [fatherland] against the anti-Patria, of national unity against separatism, of morality against iniquity, of the spirit against materialism". One of his central post-war objectives had been to maintain a festering division of Spain between the victorious and the vanquished, the privileged "authentic Spain" and the castigated "anti-Spain". For the defeated, Franco's peace meant the silence of the graveyard.

Gene Wolman was right. The people of the Spanish Republic, along with the International Brigades, had made a huge contribution to the eventual defeat of fascism. The defeated Spanish Republicans continued the fight in exile. Ten thousand died in German concentration camps. Spanish Republicans were at Narvik and at Dunkirk. They fought in North Africa and led the liberating forces into Paris. Many veterans of the International Brigades fought with distinction in the Second World War, striving to complete the task they had been unable to achieve in Spain. However, the final victory of the Allies in 1945 brought no reward for the defeated Republicans and their supporters from around the world.

The IBMT's founding president until his death in 2009 was Jack Jones, seen here in 2007 at the cemetery outside Lardero, La Rioja, for some of the more than 2,000 Republic[an] supporters murdered in th[e] province following the military coup in July 1936.

Bitterly aware of this, the British veterans, organised as the International Brigade Association, campaigned tirelessly for democracy in Spain. The IBA's declared purpose was: "To carry on in Britain the spirit and traditions of the International Brigade as front line fighters for the defence and advance of democracy against fascism, for the rapid development of common action and purpose among all anti-fascist people by spreading the truth about the struggle of the people, Army and Government of Republican Spain and to win all necessary support for the Spanish Republic." During the Second World War, the association helped Spanish veterans of the Republican cause and some International Brigaders from fascist countries who needed jobs in England.

After 1945, the IBA publicised the anti-Franco struggle and raised money in order to send British lawyers and interpreters as observers to the trials of political prisoners threatened with

the death sentence, most notably Julián Grimau and Marcos Ana in the 1960s. Their presence at least served to inhibit some of the more appalling practices of trials in which large numbers of men were often accused, tried and sentenced collectively. In late 1963 and early 1964, material and money was collected for an exhibition on the Spanish Civil War under the title "Spain Fights for Freedom". Initially intended to be small, mobile and portable, it became a large-scale enterprise, given the wealth of photographs, posters, documents and other relics with which the IBA was inundated. In 2001, the veterans of the International Brigade Association passed on the baton to the newly formed International Brigade Memorial Trust. The IBMT works both to preserve the memory of the men and women who fought in the International Brigades and in the medical and other support services in the Spanish Civil War and also to propagate the values which led them to fight. This is done by a range of publications, events and exhibitions such as *Antifascistas*.

PAUL PRESTON is Professor of Spanish History at the London School of Economics and Political Science, where he is also the Director of the Cañada Blanch Centre for Contemporary Spanish Studies. He is the author of many books on Spain and the Spanish Civil War, including the biographies *Franco: A Biography* (1993) and *Juan Carlos: A People's King* (2004) as well as *¡Comrades! Portraits from the Spanish Civil War* (1999); *Doves of War: Four Women of Spain* (2002); *The Spanish Civil War: Reaction, Revolution and Revenge* (2006) and *We Saw Spain Die: Foreign Correspondents in the Spanish Civil War* (2008).

Antifascistas

The International Brigades

International Brigade volunteers in Barcelona.

AGUSTI CENTELLES

The British Battalion banner.

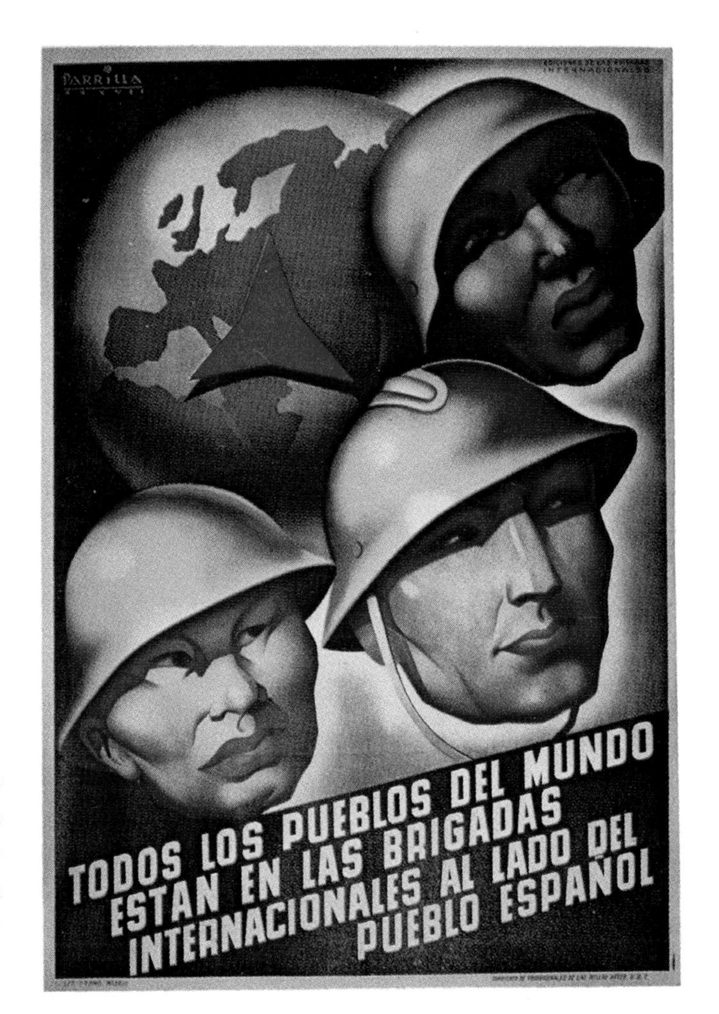

"All the peoples of the world are in the International Brigades on the side of the Spanish people," says this poster from 1937.

ON THE OUTBREAK OF WAR in Spain on 18 July 1936, volunteers from many different countries wanted to offer their support to the democratically elected Republican government. They shared the belief that they could make a difference in the fight against fascism by helping to defeat the attempted coup by right-wing forces in Spain – and, by doing so, prevent another world war.

They made their way to Barcelona and marched to the front with the newly formed militia groups. The numbers of volunteers arriving in Spain soon grew even larger when, in mid-September 1936, the Communist International – the Comintern – decided to form the International Brigades.

Recruitment for the International Brigades was carried out mainly by the Communist Party, and nearly three-quarters of the volunteers were party members. However, trade unionists, socialists and members of other left-wing groups also joined the British Battalion. Many walked across the Pyrenees at night to join other volunteers in Spain, prepared to fight despite harsh conditions and minimal pay.

The International Brigades were soon incorporated into the Spanish Republican army, the British serving mainly in the XV International Brigade. As the war continued and casualties grew ever higher, increasing numbers of Spanish recruits fought in the International Brigades alongside their foreign comrades.

Members of the British Battalion in 1938.

MARX MEMORIAL LIBRARY

tish volunteers
urning to the front
'owing convalescence
Benicasim.

X MEMORIAL LIBRARY

Spanish and German brigaders together in friendship.

Over 2,500 recruits from Britain and Ireland joined the 35,000 volunteers from 53 different countries to fight in the International Brigades. One in every five of the British volunteers died in Spain and very few escaped without some form of injury.

The majority of British volunteers were from the working class, but all classes were represented. Intellectuals, writers and poets fought side by side with volunteers from a wide variety of different occupations and from all parts of Great Britain and Ireland.

British volunteers in Barcelona in September 1936

CENTURIA INGLESA
ANTIFASCISTA
"TOM MANN"
PROLETARIA
AL

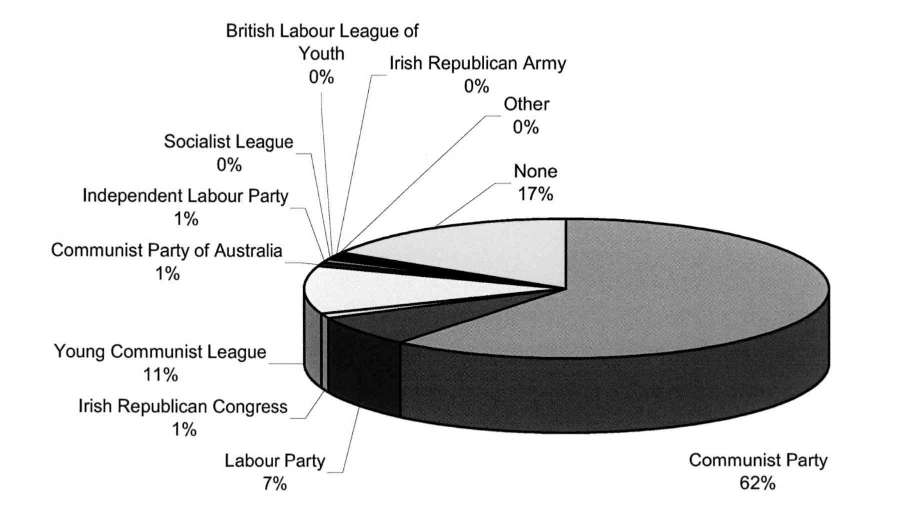

Political affiliation (where given) of the British volunteers

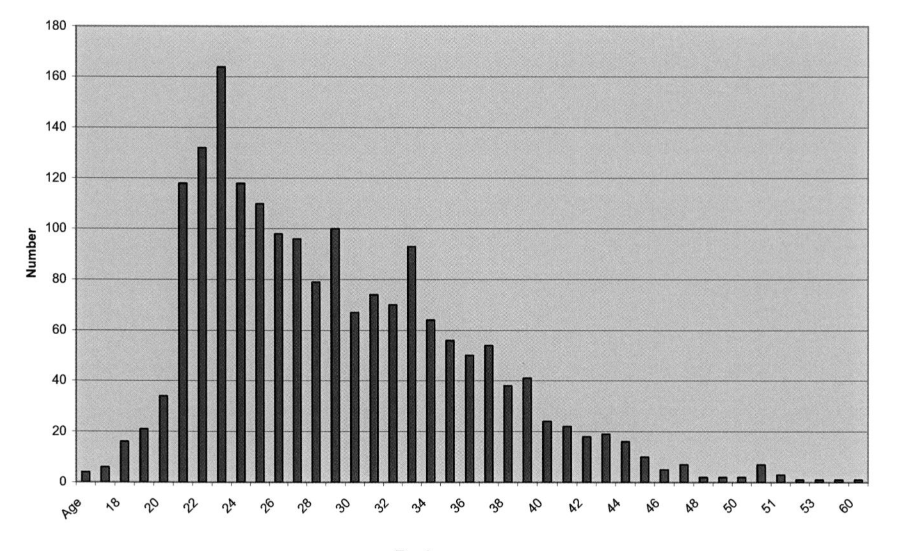

Ages of the volunteers by proportion.

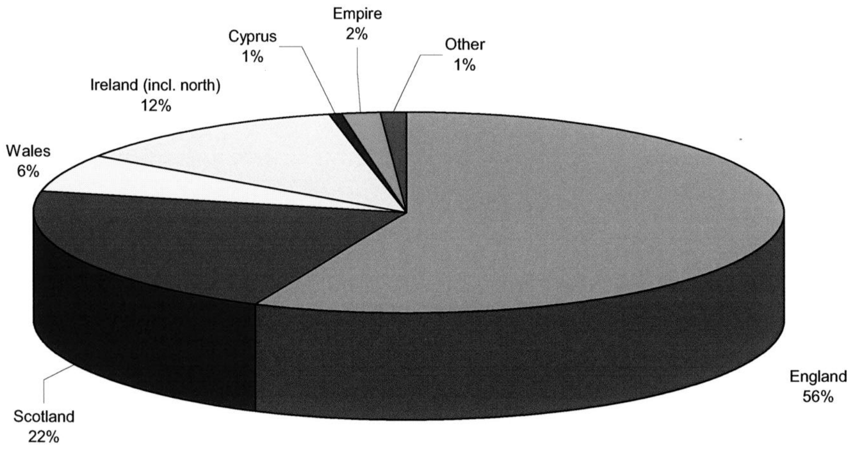

Geographical origins of the volunteers.

BRITISH MEDICAL AID

IN SPAIN

Published by THE NEWS CHRONICLE

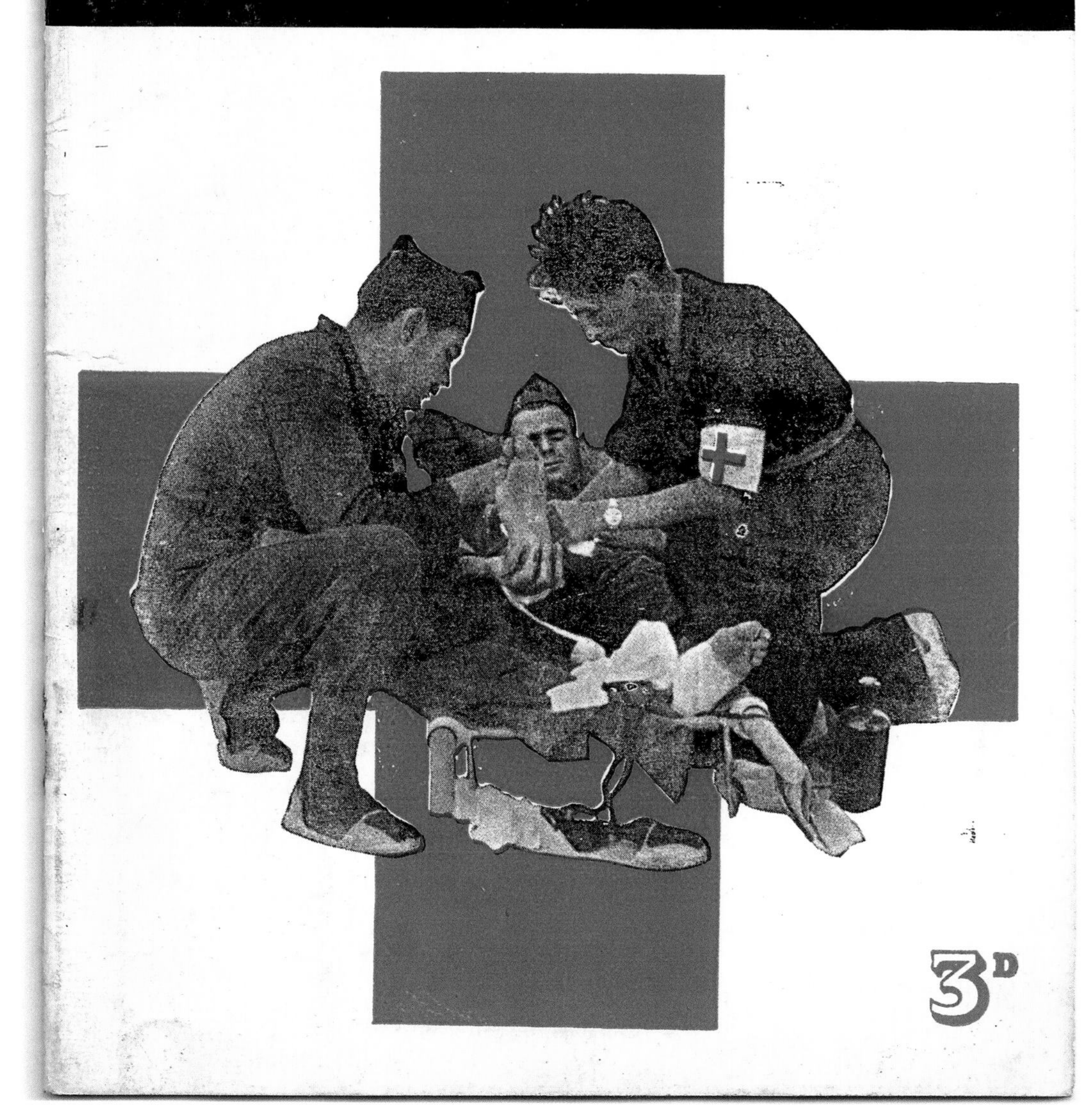

Among the volunteers were a number of medical staff.

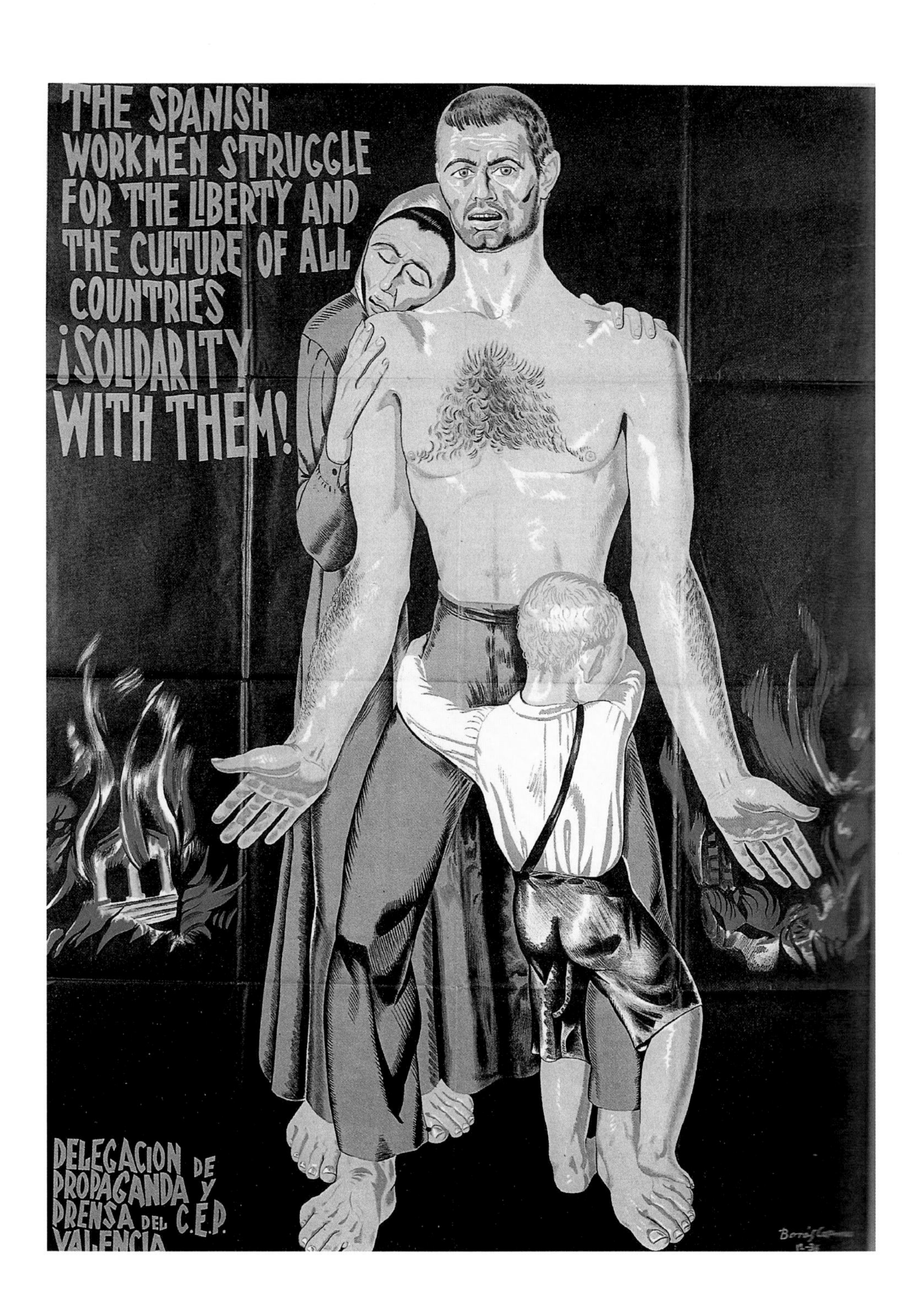
THE SPANISH WORKMEN STRUGGLE FOR THE LIBERTY AND THE CULTURE OF ALL COUNTRIES
¡SOLIDARITY WITH THEM!
DELEGACION DE PROPAGANDA Y PRENSA DEL C.E.P. VALENCIA

Antifascistas

Why They Went

FILIACION

Estatura

Pelo *moreno*

Ojos *azules*

Cara [illegible]

Barba –

Nariz

SEÑAS PARTICULARES

James R. Jump

(Firma del interesado)

Fecha de nacimiento *24/8/16*

Lugar de nacimiento *Wallasey*

Nacionalidad *Inglés*

Profesión *Obrero*

Estado civil *Soltero*

DOMICILIO: País *Inglaterra*

Pueblo *Wallasey (Cheshire)*

Calle *Parkside* núm. *32*

Partido Político *Antifascista*

Fecha de entrada en las B.I. *11/9/37*

Fecha de entrega de la libreta *24/11/38*

— 2 —

República Española

Número de la libreta *78278*

Brigadas Internacionales

CARNET MILITAR PARA

Apellidos *Jump*

Nombre *James*

LEER CON ATENCION

1) Se ruega a los camaradas que a cada cambio, su Unidad haga la inscripción correspondiente.
2) No se extienden duplicados de este Carnet.
3) Los portadores del Carnet no tienen derecho a hacer inscripciones.

— 1 —

THE SPANISH SECOND REPUBLIC, personified by La Niña Bonita [Beautiful Girl] (above) was founded on 14 April 1931 amidst scenes of popular rejoicing. However, despite the introduction of democracy, the forces of reaction continued to oppose reform as violently as they had done for over a century.

Government attempts to introduce reforms in land distribution and to limit the powers of the Catholic Church and the army provoked a powerful reactionary coalition of landowners, army officers and clergy. A new law giving women the right to vote was also opposed, as was the granting of autonomy to Catalonia in 1932 and to the Basque Country in 1936. Those on the right viewed these changes as a threat to the status quo. Meanwhile, some on the left, especially in the powerful anarchist movement, launched revolutionary actions in search of faster and more radical change.

uch needed land form was a key aim the Republic.

Antifascistas

Madrid the magnet that drew us all
Along slow roads to Spain – at last a star
For desperate men, sensing the gathering storm
And we that fought to warn a watching world
Were called false prophets by appeasers
Yet fought for the poor of the world.

From "I Sing of My Comrades"
by David Marshall (pictured),
who arrived in Spain in September 1936,
aged 20, having left his job as an
employment clerk in Middlesbrough.

JACK JONES
before the Battle of the Ebro in July 1938.

As Liverpool Labour councillor (and future general secretary of the Transport and General Workers' Union) Jack Jones, who served in Spain between March and August 1938, later explained, the desire to act came with the "awful realisation" that fascism was on the march across Europe.

"The march had started with Mussolini and had gained terrible momentum with Hitler and was being carried forward by Franco. For most young people there was a feeling of frustration, but some determined to do anything that seemed possible, even if it meant death, to try to stop the spread of fascism... This was fascist progression. It was real and it had to be stopped."

Antifascistas

Tension increased in Spain after the elections of February 1936 were won by the Popular Front, a left-wing coalition dominated by the Socialists and the Republican Left. Whilst the coalition gained a clear majority of seats in the parliament, their victory was narrow in terms of votes. Political rhetoric became increasingly polarised and violent outbreaks continued on the streets and in the countryside.

Popular Front candidates for Madrid.

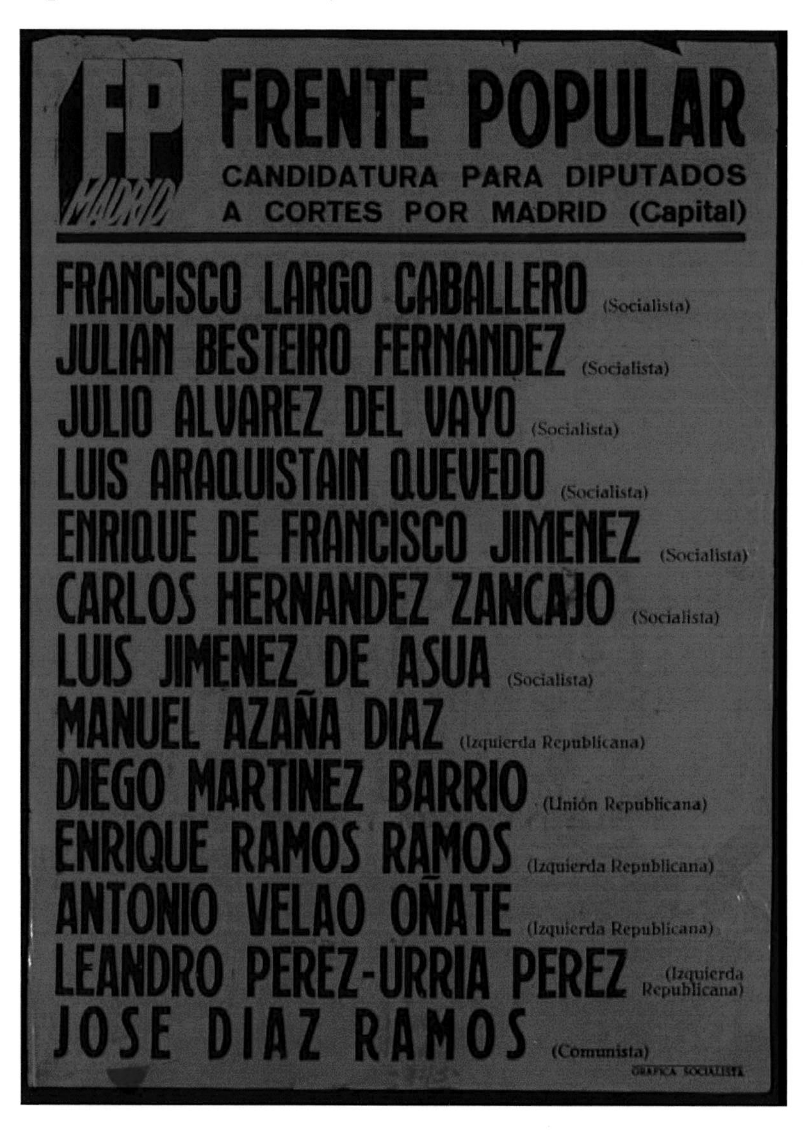

Crowds celebrati
in Madrid's Plaza
Cibeles following t
Popular Front victory
February 19

ARCHIVO GENERAL
LA ADMINISTRAC

Antifascistas

An uprising led by right-wing generals on 17-18 July 1936 began as a carefully planned coup, but was strongly resisted by forces loyal to the Republic. People on the left joined militia groups that were swiftly organised by various political parties and trade unions.

The attempted coup provoked a collapse of the state apparatus in many parts of Spain and violent revenge was exacted upon organisations and individuals that supported the coup, particularly the Church. It took some months before the Republican government was able to regain control and put an

The poster and banner across a Madrid street say: "They shall not pass!"

Militiaman and woman at watch on the front in late July 1936.

ARCHIVO GENERAL DE LA ADMINISTRACIÓN

end to the violence. By contrast, in the areas of Spain conquered by the rebel generals, a deliberate and systematic repression was ruthlessly applied against all perceived supporters of the Republic – a strategy that was to be continued long after the war had finished.

The tide began to turn when General Francisco Franco brought the Army of Africa over to mainland Spain from Spanish Morocco in early August. His success in obtaining help from Nazi Germany and Fascist Italy to airlift 15,000 battle-hardened troops across the Strait of Gibraltar was crucial to the military rebels' chances of victory. Franco was soon receiving huge supplies of armaments and ammunition from both Germany and Italy. For Hitler, the war in Spain offered a training ground for the Condor Legion, a specialised unit equipped with the latest German bombers and fighter aircraft. Meanwhile, Mussolini sent around 80,000 soldiers to fight alongside Franco's troops. The situation had escalated from a civil war to a conflict with an international dimension.

Those who volunteered to serve in the International Brigades were united in the belief that they should help the Spanish people in their fight to defend democracy – and in their opposition to fascism. They were aware of the dangers posed by the rise to power of the dictators in Germany and Italy, where the politics of repression – towards political opponents, trade unions, Jews and other minorities – was already causing fear and suffering. Thousands fled for their lives into exile; some became members of the International Brigades.

Opposite, above: Franco's Moroccan troops being airlifted to mainland Spain.

Opposite, below: Victims of an air-raid by the rebels on Republican-held Barcelona. MARX MEMORIAL LIBRARY

Antifascistas

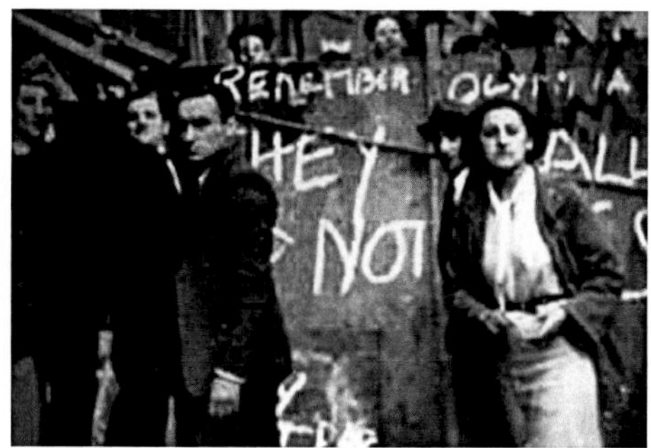

Opponents of Mosley at Cable Street.

In Britain, the leader of the British Union of Fascists, Sir Oswald Mosley (above), was gathering a degree of support on the right with his militaristic style and anti-Semitic rhetoric. The members of his party, known as "Blackshirts", were notorious for their violence at meetings towards anyone who spoke out against them. On 4 October 1936, Mosley and his Blackshirts attempted to parade through the East End of London. Thousands of ordinary people blocked the streets and successfully prevented them from marching, chanting the same slogan as the people in the streets of Madrid: "¡No pasarán!" – "They shall not pass!" A number of those who opposed the fascists that day, which came to be known as the Battle of

LOU KENTON,
from Stepney, took part in the Battle of Cable Street and afterwards rode his motorcycle to Spain, arriving in February 1937, where he worked as a messenger and ambulance driver. He was one of several Jewish communists from the East End who joined the International Brigades. Between 10-20 per cent of the 2,500 volunteers from the British Isles are thought to have been Jewish.

Cartoon by David Low from the Evening Standard *of 23 December 1936.*

Benito Mussolini and Adolf Hitler.

Cable Street, also volunteered for the International Brigades.

The British government, faced with the expansionist ambitions of Hitler and Mussolini, decided to avoid open conflict and instead tried to appease the dictators. When the war began in Spain, both France and Britain promoted a policy of non-intervention which had disastrous results for the Republic. The London-based Non-Intervention Committee was a sham, turning a blind eye to the soldiers and armaments supplied to Franco by Germany and Italy, whilst refusing to allow the Republicans their legal right to buy arms. Although most of the British establishment was hoping for a Franco victory, many ordinary British people were determined to show their support for the Republic and thousands of grass-roots campaigns were organised to send aid to the Spanish people.

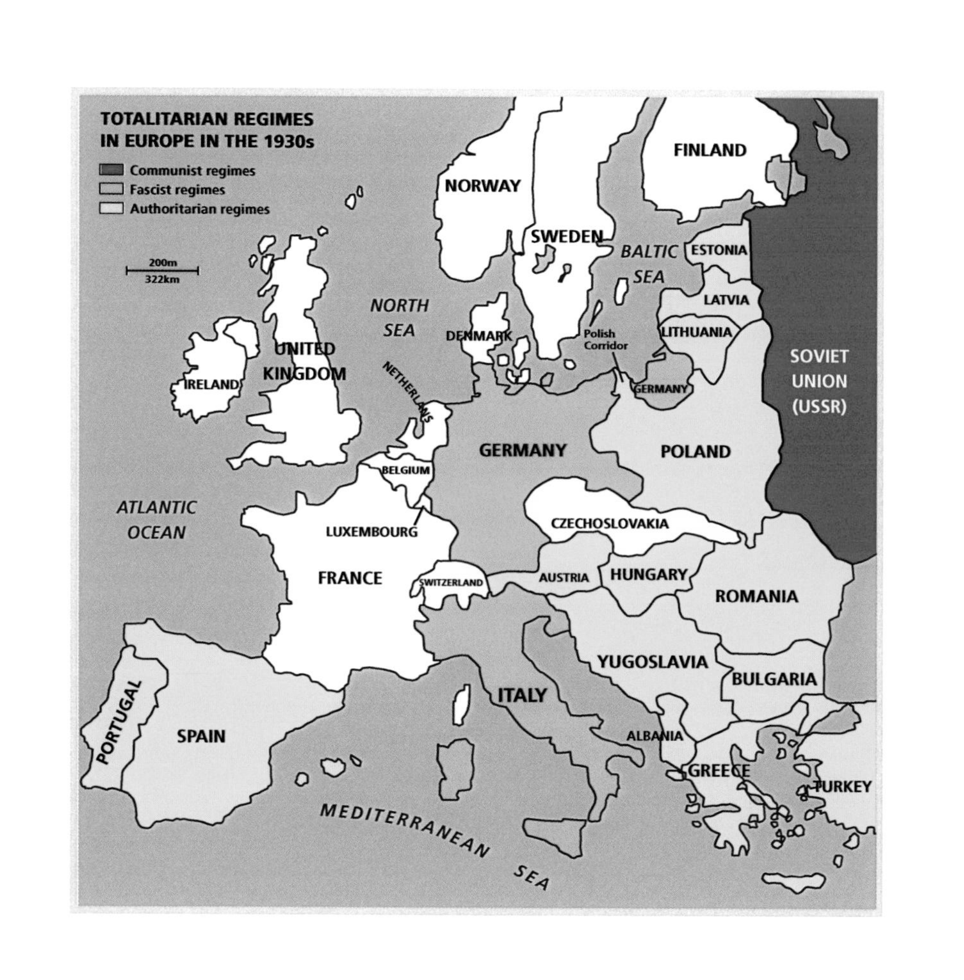
TOTALITARIAN REGIMES
IN EUROPE IN THE 1930s
Communist regimes
Fascist regimes
Authoritarian regimes
200m
322km
NORWAY
SWEDEN
FINLAND
ESTONIA
LATVIA
LITHUANIA
BALTIC
SEA
NORTH
SEA
DENMARK
Polish
Corridor
GERMANY
UNITED
KINGDOM
IRELAND
NETHERLANDS
BELGIUM
LUXEMBOURG
GERMANY
POLAND
SOVIET
UNION
(USSR)
ATLANTIC
OCEAN
FRANCE
SWITZERLAND
CZECHOSLOVAKIA
AUSTRIA
HUNGARY
ROMANIA
YUGOSLAVIA
BULGARIA
ITALY
ALBANIA
GREECE
TURKEY
PORTUGAL
SPAIN
MEDITERRANEAN
SEA

Antifascistas

Key Battles

Commemorative plate produced by the International Brigade Association.

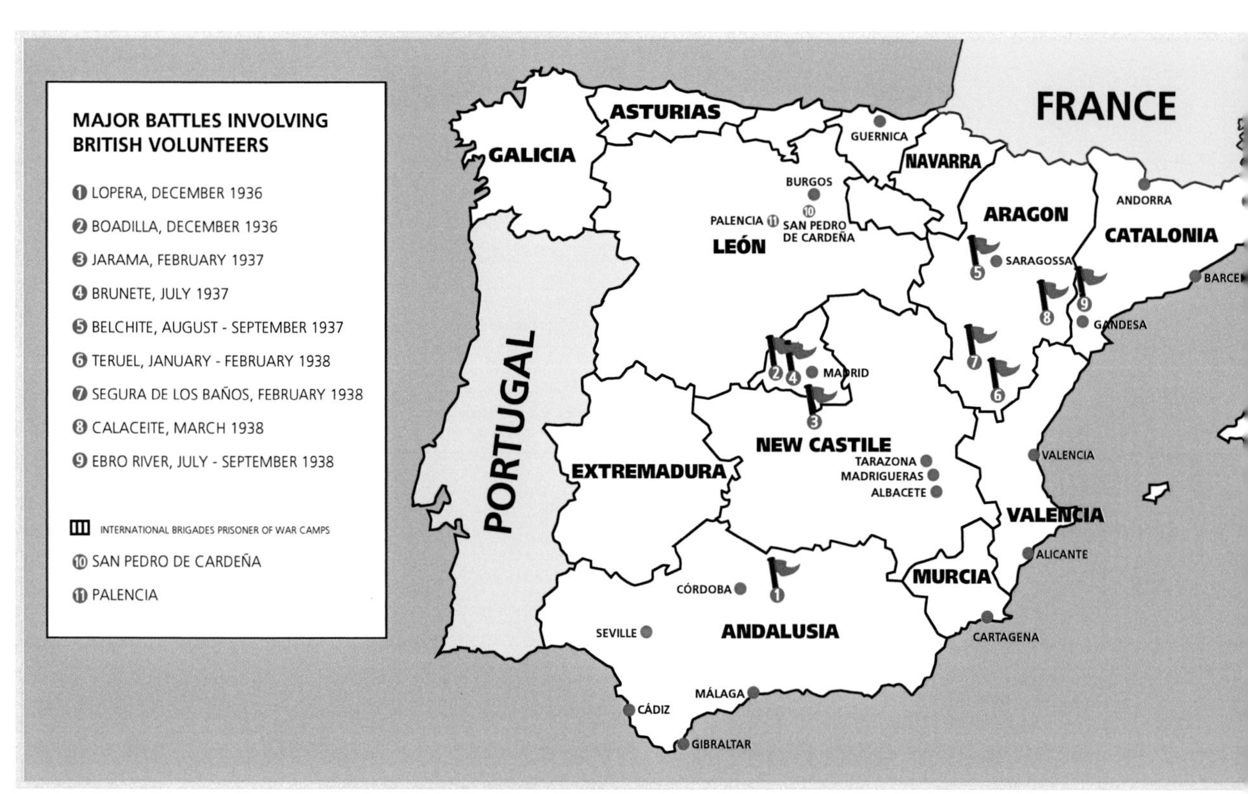
MAJOR BATTLES INVOLVING BRITISH VOLUNTEERS
❶ LOPERA, DECEMBER 1936
❷ BOADILLA, DECEMBER 1936
❸ JARAMA, FEBRUARY 1937
❹ BRUNETE, JULY 1937
❺ BELCHITE, AUGUST - SEPTEMBER 1937
❻ TERUEL, JANUARY - FEBRUARY 1938
❼ SEGURA DE LOS BAÑOS, FEBRUARY 1938
❽ CALACEITE, MARCH 1938
❾ EBRO RIVER, JULY - SEPTEMBER 1938
INTERNATIONAL BRIGADES PRISONER OF WAR CAMPS
⑩ SAN PEDRO DE CARDEÑA
⑪ PALENCIA
FRANCE
ASTURIAS
GALICIA
GUERNICA
NAVARRA
BURGOS
PALENCIA
SAN PEDRO DE CARDEÑA
LEÓN
ARAGON
ANDORRA
CATALONIA
SARAGOSSA
GANDESA
PORTUGAL
MADRID
NEW CASTILE
EXTREMADURA
TARAZONA
MADRIGUERAS
ALBACETE
VALENCIA
VALENCIA
ALICANTE
MURCIA
CÓRDOBA
SEVILLE
ANDALUSIA
CARTAGENA
MÁLAGA
CÁDIZ
GIBRALTAR

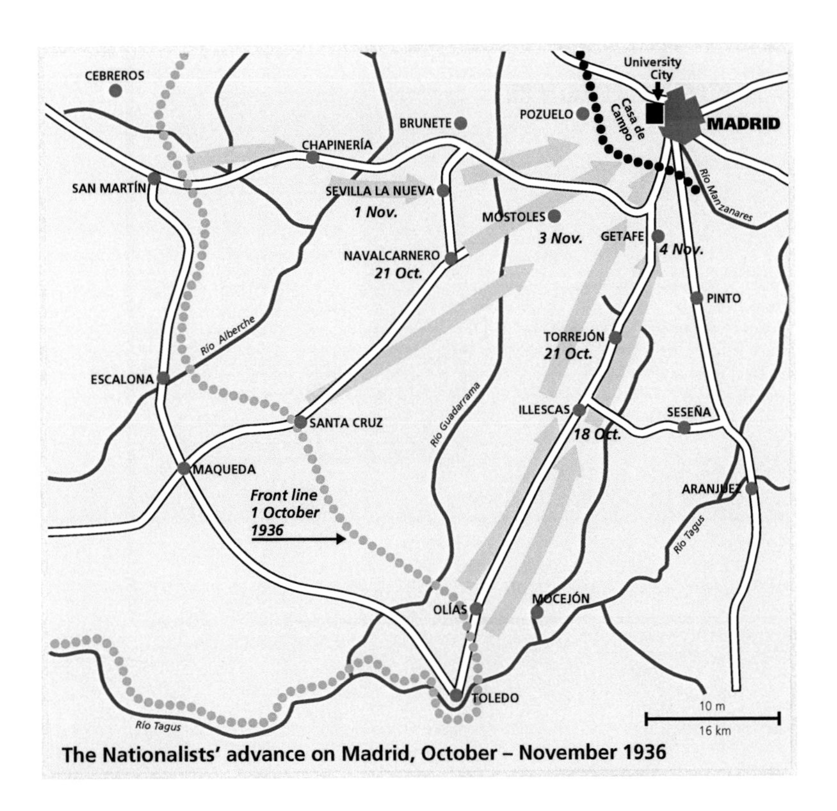

The Nationalists' advance on Madrid, October – November 1936

Madrid

BY EARLY NOVEMBER 1936 the rebel army had reached the south-western suburbs of Madrid and the Republican government was so convinced that Madrid would fall that it moved to Valencia to be able to continue the fight. However, with the newly arrived XI International Brigade and the Communist Party's Fifth Regiment, the population of Madrid embarked on a desperate defence. They were helped by military aid from the Soviet Union, which had agreed to sell arms to the Republic after realising that the policy of non-intervention was being brazenly flouted by Hitler and Mussolini. There was hand-to-hand fighting as Franco's Moroccan troops almost reached the city centre, but the defenders drove them back. By the end of November, the attack was spent and the capital, for the moment, held out.

La Coruña road

The following month, in December 1936, the Nationalists, as Franco's rebels and their supporters were now calling themselves, began an attempt to cut the Madrid-La Coruña road to the north-west of the capital. After heavy losses in fighting around the village of Boadilla – vividly described by Esmond Romilly in his book of the same name – the attack was called off. On 5 January 1937 the assault was renewed and during four days of fighting, for very little strategic gain by the Nationalists, each side lost in the region of 15,000 men. Casualties among the International Brigades were particularly high.

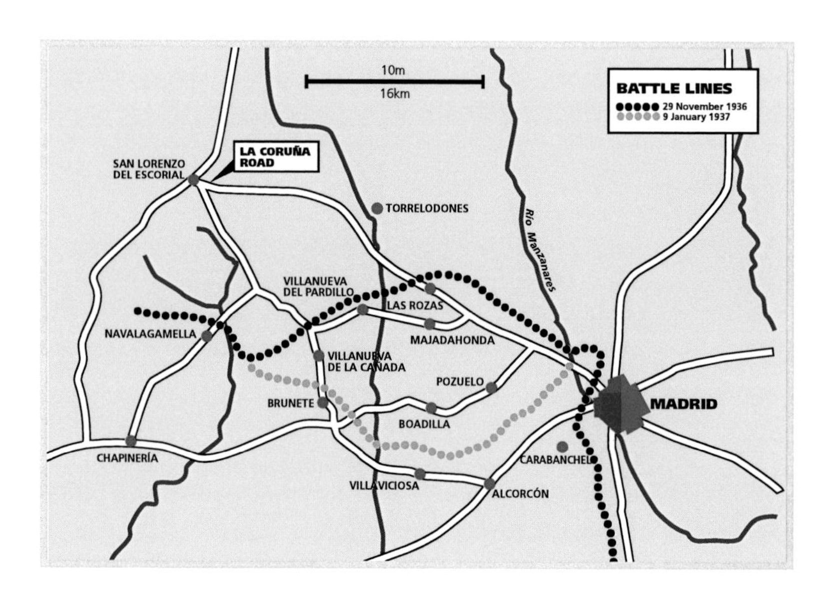

ESMOND ROMILLY, the 17-year-old nephew of Winston Churchill, fought in Spain between October and December 1936 and later wrote of his experiences fighting near Madrid in *Boadilla*.

Whilst at public school Romilly produced a newspaper called "Out of Bounds" which carried articles about the threat of fascism and whether or not to join the Officer Training Corps (OTC) to pick up the skills necessary for fighting in the revolution. A rather progressive paper, it dealt with masturbation and homosexuality in public schools.

Esmond's elder brother Giles also fought in Spain, arriving in January 1937. Both survived their Spanish episode, though Esmond was killed during the Second World War whilst serving as a bomber pilot.

Until the end of 1936, the small numbers of British and Irish volunteers fighting in Madrid's University City and Casa de Campo were included with French or German units; likewise, the English-speaking No.1 Company – which fought at Lopera, near Córdoba, and at Las Rozas on the outskirts of Madrid – was part of the Marseillaise Battalion, XIV International Brigade. However, by Christmas 1936 there were enough volunteers at the International Brigade base at Albacete, midway between Madrid and Valencia, to form the British Battalion. The volunteers were transferred to the nearby village of Madrigueras for training, which remained the British base until July 1937, when it was transferred to Tarazona de la Mancha.

The British Battalion's makeshift kitchen.

MARX MEMORIAL LIBRARY

Jarama

In February 1937 the Nationalists made a renewed attempt to surround Madrid by cutting the road to Valencia, to the south of the Spanish capital, in the Battle of Jarama. Republican troops reinforced by International Brigades were thrown into the defence. They held on desperately, checking the rebels' advance, but at great cost. The Republicans lost at least 10,000 dead and wounded and the Nationalists 6,000. Of the 500 that had gone into battle with the British Battalion on the first day of fighting, as many as 136 were killed and a similar number wounded, leaving less than half the battalion unscathed. Thirty members of the Machine-Gun Company were captured, with three prisoners shot out of hand. The commander, Harold Fry, only survived because his officer's markings had been ripped from his uniform by his quick-thinking adjutant when they were captured.

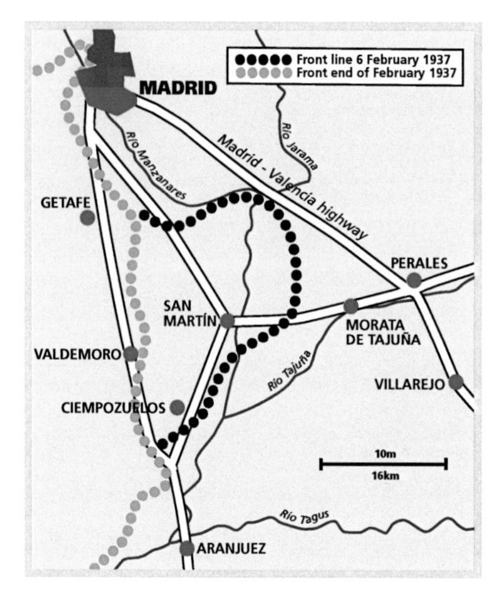

Rebels' attempt to encircle Madrid, February 1937.

The British Battalion at Jarama.

MARX MEMORIAL LIBRARY

Members of the British Battalion's Machine-Gun Company captured at Jarama. Harold Fry, company commander, is seventh from the right. MARX MEMORIAL LIBRARY

The 33-year-old Communist Party member **HAROLD FRY** arrived in Spain in December 1936, having served previously as a sergeant with the British Army in China.

Fry was the commander of the Machine-Gun Company at Jarama where he was wounded in the arm and captured on 13 February 1937. Like many of his comrades, Fry was sentenced to death, but was exchanged for a Nationalist prisoner in May 1937 and repatriated back to Britain.

Fry returned to Spain in August and was eventually made British Battalion commander. He was killed by shellfire on 13 October 1937 at Fuentes de Ebro.

The Republican offensive at Brunete. MARX MEMORIAL LIBRARY

Brunete

In March 1937, the Republican army scored a spectacular success when it routed Italian forces at Guadalajara. But success was short-lived, for in June Bilbao and the Basque Country fell to the advancing Nationalist forces. The Republic responded by launching a major offensive at Brunete, to the west of Madrid, on 6 July 1937, designed to relieve pressure on the northern front and break through the rebels at their weakest point. The XV International Brigade, supported by the fledgling British Anti-Tank Battery under the command of the gifted leader and military strategist Malcolm Dunbar, was heavily involved in the capture of Villanueva de la Cañada, which lay in between the Republicans and their target of Brunete and the heights overlooking Madrid. However, despite initial Republican gains, Franco was able to bring his superior numbers to bear and gradually pushed back the Republican forces.

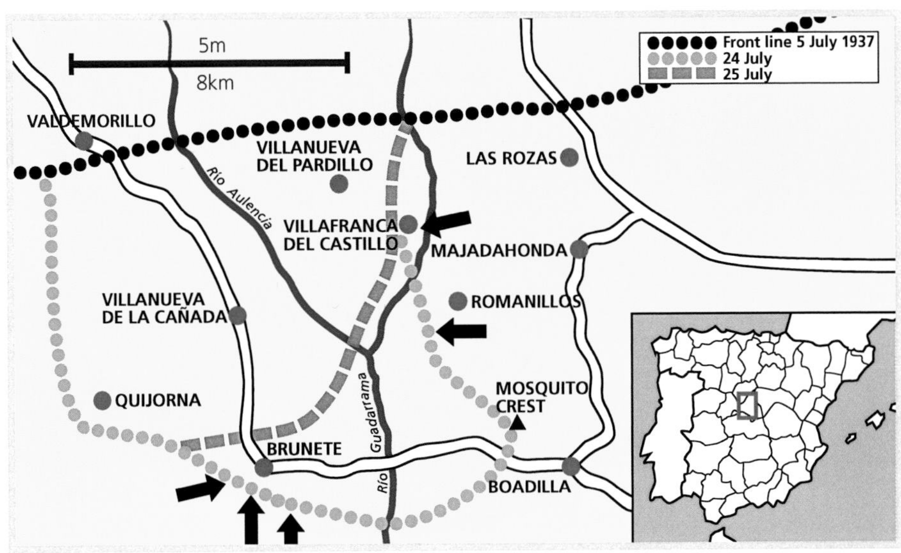

The Battle of Brunete, July 1937.

British volunteers at an advance dressing station at Brunete in July 1937.

MARX MEMORIAL LIBRARY

Aragon: August – October 1937

Aragon

With the failure of the Brunete offensive, Franco was able to continue with his northern operation, and Santander fell to the rebels at the end of August 1937. Again the Republicans tried to divert attention from the northern front by launching an offensive in Aragon aimed at capturing Saragossa. Though inroads were made – International Brigades were heavily involved in capturing Quinto and Belchite despite heavy casualties – Saragossa remained in rebel hands and Asturias, the last part of Republican-held Spain in the north, fell to the rebels in October 1937. The loss of the northern Atlantic ports and the area's vital heavy industries was a crucial blow to the Republic.

The British Anti-Tank Battery in late 1937. MARX MEMORIAL LIBRARY

Born in Paignton, Devon, in 1912, **MALCOLM DUNBAR** read Economics and History at Trinity College, Cambridge. Whilst working as a journalist, he was arrested at the Battle of Cable Street in October 1936.

Dunbar arrived in Spain in January 1937 and due to his OTC experience was quickly promoted to section leader. He was wounded at the Battle of Jarama the following month.

Described by a colleague as "a courageous intellectual", Dunbar was appointed the first commander of the elite British Anti-Tank Battery when it was created in June 1937. A talented officer, he replaced the American Bob Merriman as chief of staff for the entire XV International Brigade in April 1938 and was promoted to major in October at its farewell parade. The commander of the American Lincoln Battalion, Milton Wolff, remembered Dunbar as one of the two best soldiers in the brigade.

During the Second World War Dunbar was admitted into the British Army as a private in the summer of 1940. He was eventually promoted to sergeant in an armoured unit in 1942 but, despite his unquestionable experience, he never rose any higher up the ranks.

Teruel

Despite the losses in the north, the Republic was able to launch a surprise attack in December 1937, which successfully captured the city of Teruel. In freezing winter conditions the Republic's best troops, including the International Brigades and the Fifth Regiment, fought desperately but were unable to prevent Franco bringing his superior numbers of arms and men to bear. The Nationalists recaptured Teruel in February 1938. The British suffered heavy casualties and morale received a further hammer blow when one of the battalion was executed after attempting to desert to the rebels.

Though the International Brigades were an army of volunteers, they were nevertheless under military discipline whilst serving in the Spanish Republican Army. On occasions, this could be strictly and brutally applied. "**ALLAN KEMP**" (a pseudonym) left his home in Glasgow – and his wife and two children – to fight in Spain. He arrived in October 1937 and was made a sergeant in No.1 Company of the British Battalion. In December 1937 he and another British volunteer were captured by Republican soldiers, whilst attempting to desert across to the Nationalist lines carrying plans of the International Brigade positions.

Kemp's companion was sent to a punishment battalion and was later killed by shellfire. However, as the older man and senior in rank, Kemp was held responsible and was executed on 20 January 1938.

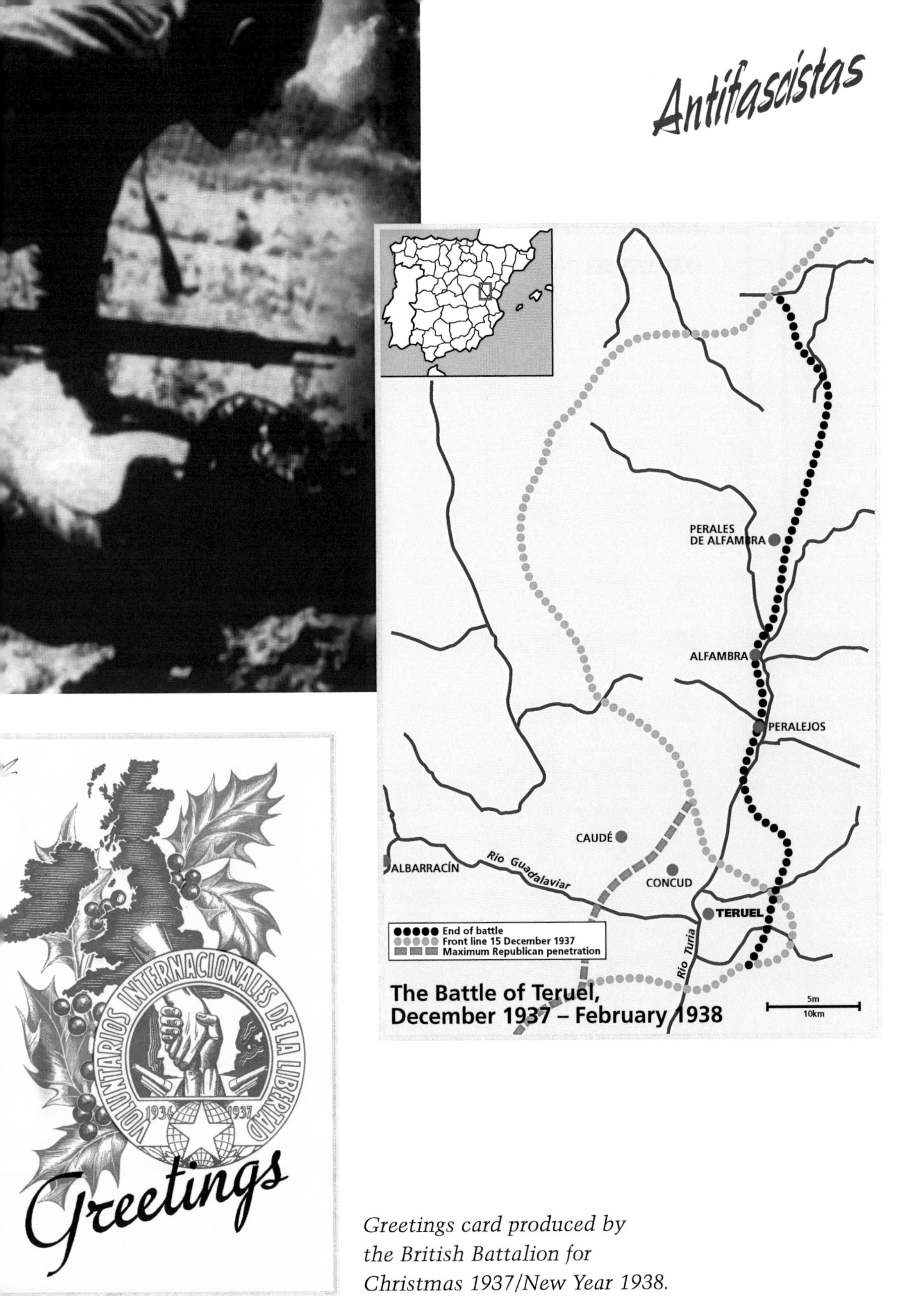

Greetings card produced by the British Battalion for Christmas 1937/New Year 1938.

Aragon retreats

Boosted by the recapture of Teruel, Franco launched a massive and well prepared attack in Aragon on 7 March 1938, involving 100,000 men, 200 tanks and over 600 Italian and German planes. What began as a series of breakthroughs for the Nationalists swiftly became outright retreat for the exhausted Republican forces, as their lines virtually collapsed under the ferocious and well-supplied offensive. Amongst many British killed in the retreats was Walter Tapsell, their popular political commissar. A large number were captured at Calaceite and imprisoned, including the influential Irish leader, Frank Ryan.

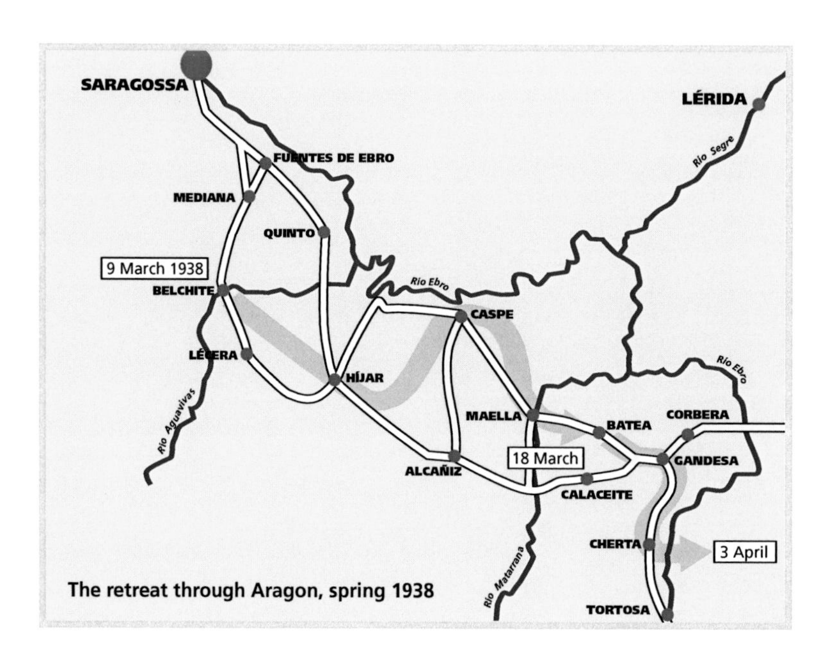

The retreat through Aragon, spring 1938

WALTER TAPSELL had been the circulation manager of the communist daily paper, the *Daily Worker*. At 34 years of age, he was a former leader of the Young Communist League and was an experienced and trusted Communist Party official. He had studied at the Lenin School in Moscow and was a member of the party's central committee from 1928–33.

Tapsell arrived in Spain in March 1937 and worked at the International Brigade base at Albacete before joining the battalion in May 1937. He was commended for his work during the Battle of Teruel. He was the British Battalion's political commissar during the retreats in the spring of 1938 and was killed at Calaceite on 1 April 1938 whilst trying to shoot an Italian tank commander still in his tank.

The assessment of Tapsell by his superiors in Spain read: "Politically sound. Militarily ambitious and is too prone to take over military commander's duties. Strong character but finds it difficult to work collectively with other comrades. Strong individualistic tendencies. Personally courageous."

FRANK RYAN, from Limerick and a former student of University College, Dublin, was a senior and influential figure in the Irish Republican movement.

He arrived in Spain in December 1936 and was wounded in the arm at the Battle of Jarama, where he played an instrumental role in rallying the exhausted and dispirited remainder of the British Battalion on the third desperate day of the fighting.

Ryan was captured at Calaceite in March 1938 and imprisoned in the concentration camp at San Pedro de Cardeña, near Burgos. Eventually he was released and transferred to Germany following a request from the German Foreign Office, who hoped to make use of him and his influence with the Irish nationalist movement. The exact details of Ryan's period in Germany remain ambiguous and he never returned to Ireland, dying in Dresden in June 1944.

Republican forces launch their offensive across the Ebro in the summer of 1938. MARX MEMORIAL LIBRA

By 15 April 1938, the rebels had reached the Mediterranean and cut the Republic in two. Had Franco headed north into Catalonia he would probably have ended the war a year earlier than he did. However, his aim was not just to defeat the Republic, but to annihilate it forever.

The Ebro

Three months after the Aragon retreats, in July 1938, the Republic launched what would become the last throw of the dice when its forces advanced back across the River Ebro and attacked Gandesa. The British Battalion was now under the

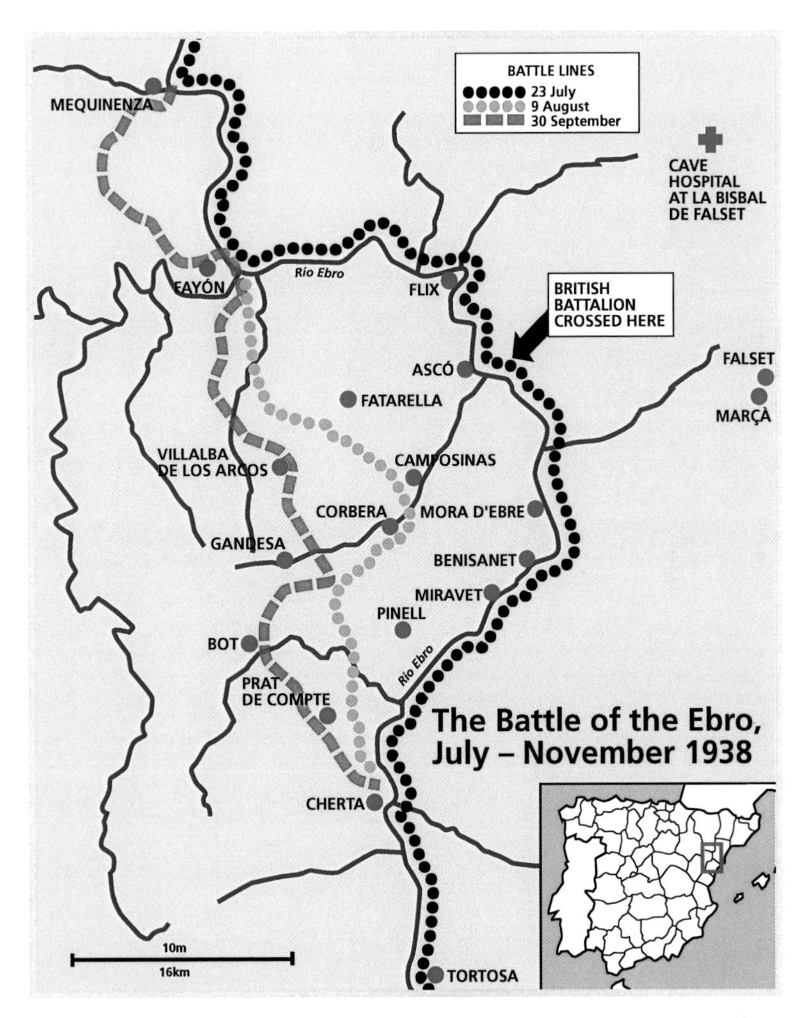

The British Battalion at Hill 481, near Gandesa.

MARX MEMORIAL LIBRARY

command of two of its most talented and experienced leaders: commander Sam Wild and political commissar Bob Cooney. But, in a familiar story for the Republican forces, initial successes soon ground to a halt when they were faced by the Nationalists' hugely superior numbers and armaments. The Battle of the Ebro lasted for over three months until, bled to death, the Republican army essentially collapsed.

The British Battalion at the Ebro.

MARX MEMORIAL LIBRARY

Before his time in Spain, the self-proclaimed "natural rebel" **SAM WILD** had been active in the National Unemployed Workers' Movement and in anti-Mosley protests in Manchester. He volunteered for Spain in January 1937 with his brother-in-law Bert Maisky, who was killed the following month in the Battle of Jarama.

Initially elected battalion armourer, Wild became a company commander in July 1937, before taking full command of the British Battalion on 17 February 1938.

"Firm and cool-headed" under fire, he was one of the best and bravest of the commanders of the battalion and was wounded three times during his time in Spain. He was decorated with the Medal of Valour for his actions during the Ebro offensive and promoted to the rank of major at the final parade of the Spanish Republican army's 35th Division in October 1938.

Despite his exemplary record in Spain, when the Second World War broke out Wild was deemed "undesirable" by Manchester's chief constable and refused admission into the British Army.

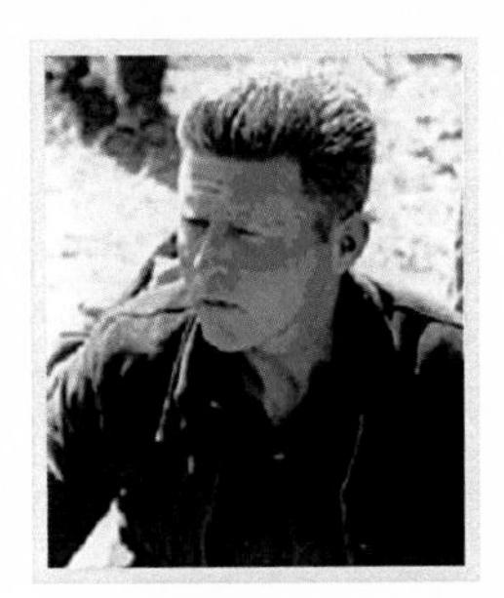

The leading Aberdeen Communist Party member, **BOB COONEY**, had a long history of activism in the party. Originally seen as too valuable to volunteer, he was eventually given permission to go to Spain and arrived in October 1937, though he didn't actually join the British Battalion until January-February 1938.

Cooney's political experience and authority – he had spent a year training at the Lenin School in Moscow in 1934 – made him an ideal candidate to replace Walter Tapsell as battalion political commissar when Tapsell was killed in April 1938. He later became commissar for the entire XV International Brigade. A report by his superiors described Cooney as "the best commissar we have", saying that he was "irreproachable", with the capacity to show initiative and react promptly to problems.

Cooney was repatriated to Britain with the other surviving volunteers at the end of 1938.

Part of the British Battalion before going into battle in July 1938. MARX MEMORIAL LIBRARY

Antifascistas

Medical Aid for Spain

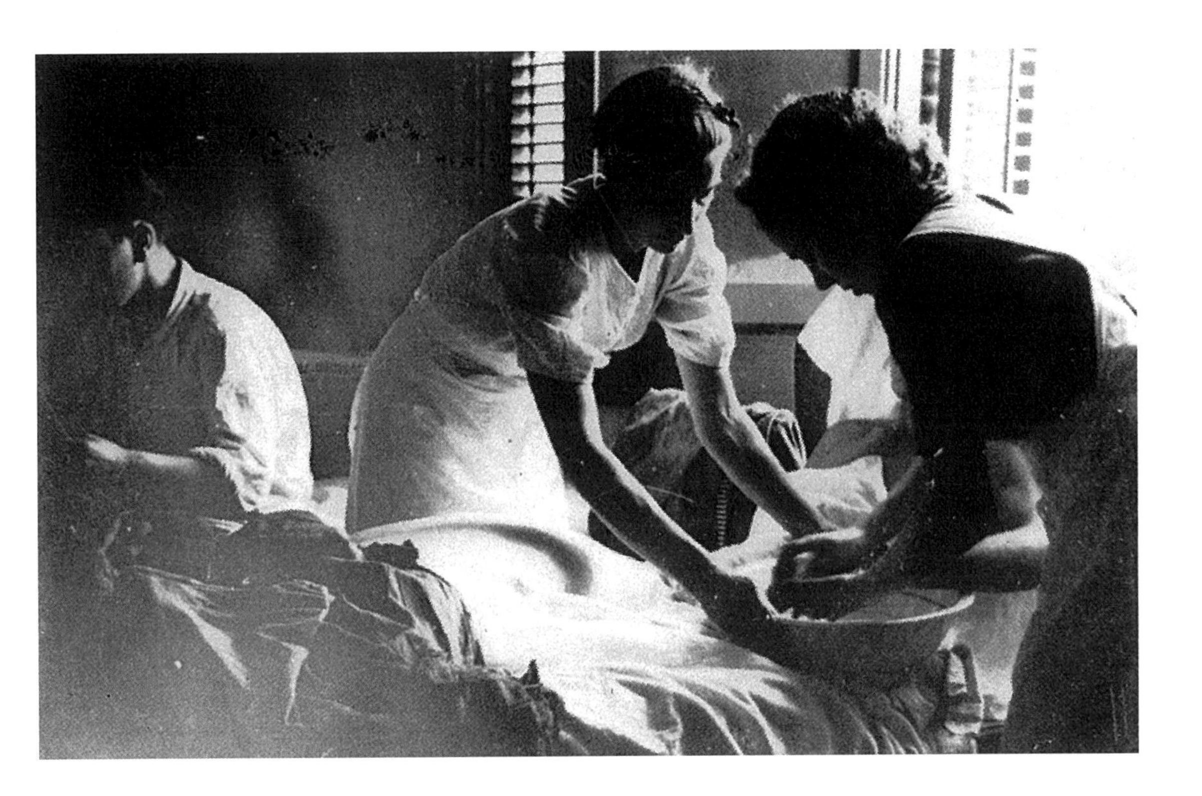

Patience Darton training a Spanish girl in nursing techniques in Valls, 1938.

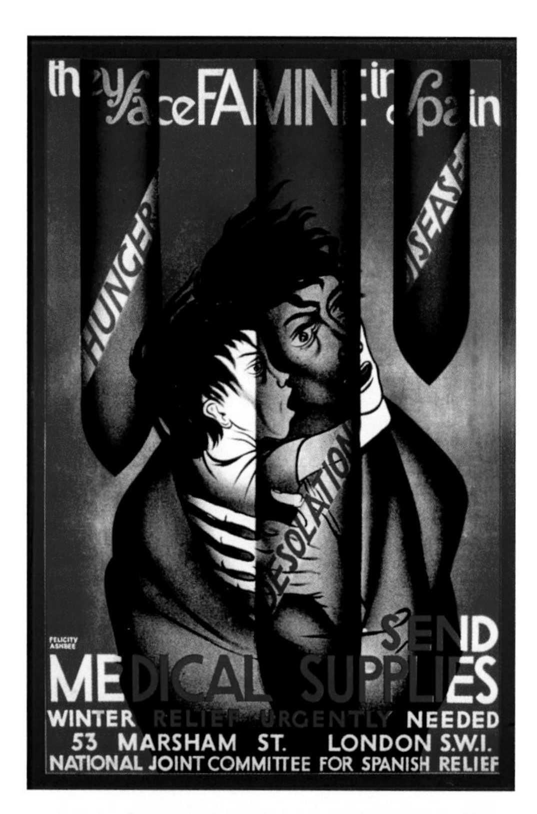

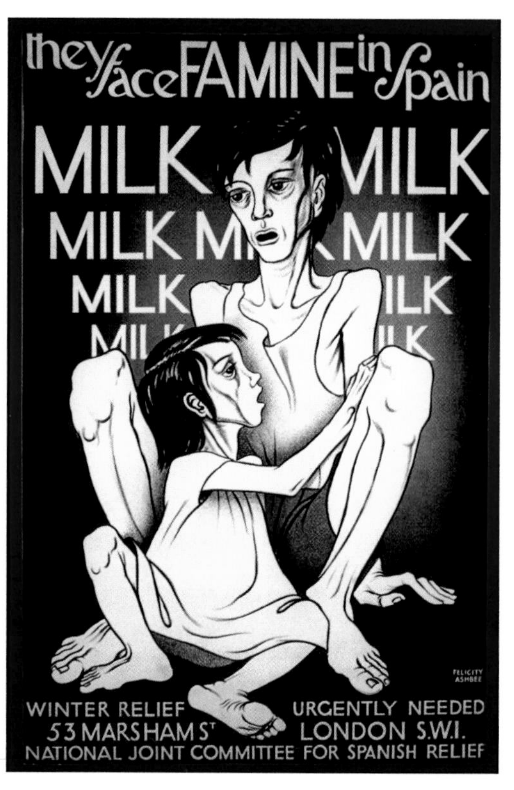

Posters by Felicity Ashbee.

DESPITE the British government's policy of non-intervention, polls taken showed that there was overwhelming support among the British people for the Spanish Republic. Committees sprang up throughout the country, involving people from all walks of life. Although left-wing activists were in the majority, the campaigns attracted support from a wide political spectrum.

Within the extraordinary diversity of local groups making up this "Aid Spain" movement, many were raising money specifically for ambulances, medical equipment, supplies and staff.

Ambulance supplied by a British aid organisation being unloaded at Dieppe.

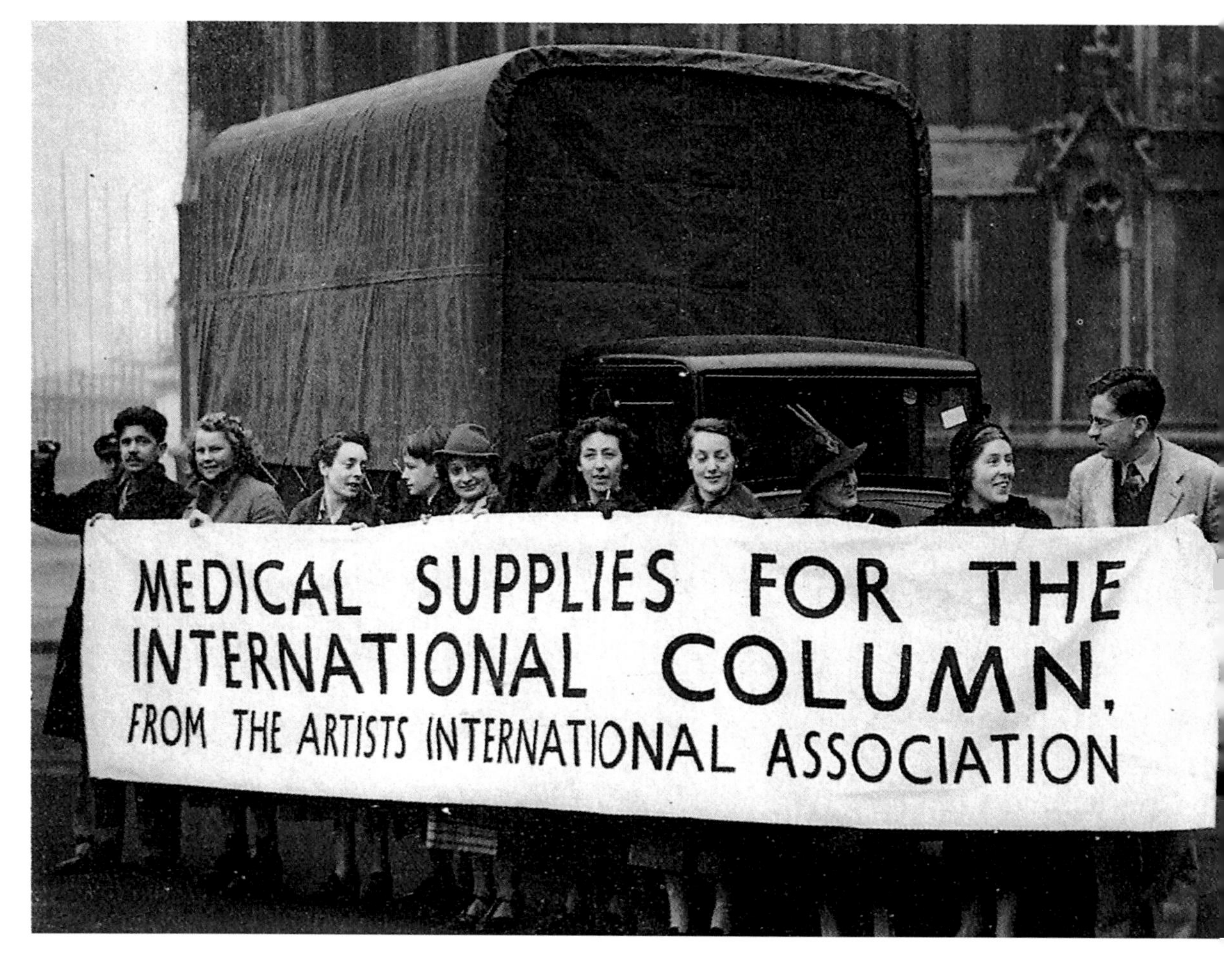

Artists International Association group with lorry containing medical supplies for Spain.

MARX MEMORIAL LIBRA

The First British Medical Unit leaves for Spain.

A number of British doctors and ambulance drivers, and dozens of nurses, volunteered to serve in the provisional hospitals organised by the Spanish Medical Aid Committee in London, and later with the International Brigades.

When the first British Medical Unit left for Spain on 23 August 1936, huge crowds gathered at London's Victoria Station to bid them farewell. As local mayors in full regalia made speeches to wish them well, the newsreel cameras recorded the event for posterity.

From the Daily Worker, *3 January 1938:*
"Four British nurses left Victoria Station on Friday night to return, after a short Christmas leave, to their work on the Aragon and other Spanish fronts. Theirs is a grim job, for they handle the worst cases, straight from the line, in mobile dressing stations. Their work is done in face of great difficulty and often hardship. But they smile happily because they are glad to be able to take part in the fight for democracy. They are extra cheerful on this trip since they are carrying with them the gramophones and books generously given by Daily Worker readers."

Thora Silverthorne and Dr Alex Tudor H
operating near the front in 19

MARX MEMORIAL LIBR

"Auto-chir" lorries.

During the Spanish Civil War, medical units with the Republican army were working closer to the front than ever before in an assortment of hastily converted buildings. Mobile units were organised using lorries known as "auto-chirs", specially equipped to act as operating theatres wherever needed. New techniques of "triage" helped save lives by identifying the cases in need of urgent attention.

Revolutionary methods in the treatment of open fractures led to a marked reduction in the numbers of amputations.

Some of the nurses, like Thora Silverthorne (opposite, above), were already politically active before they volunteered for Spain. Others, like Penny Phelps (right), who worked with the Italian International Brigaders – the "Garibaldis" – had little involvement with politics before going to Spain.

Penny Phelps and villagers at Quintan

MARX MEMORIAL LIBRA

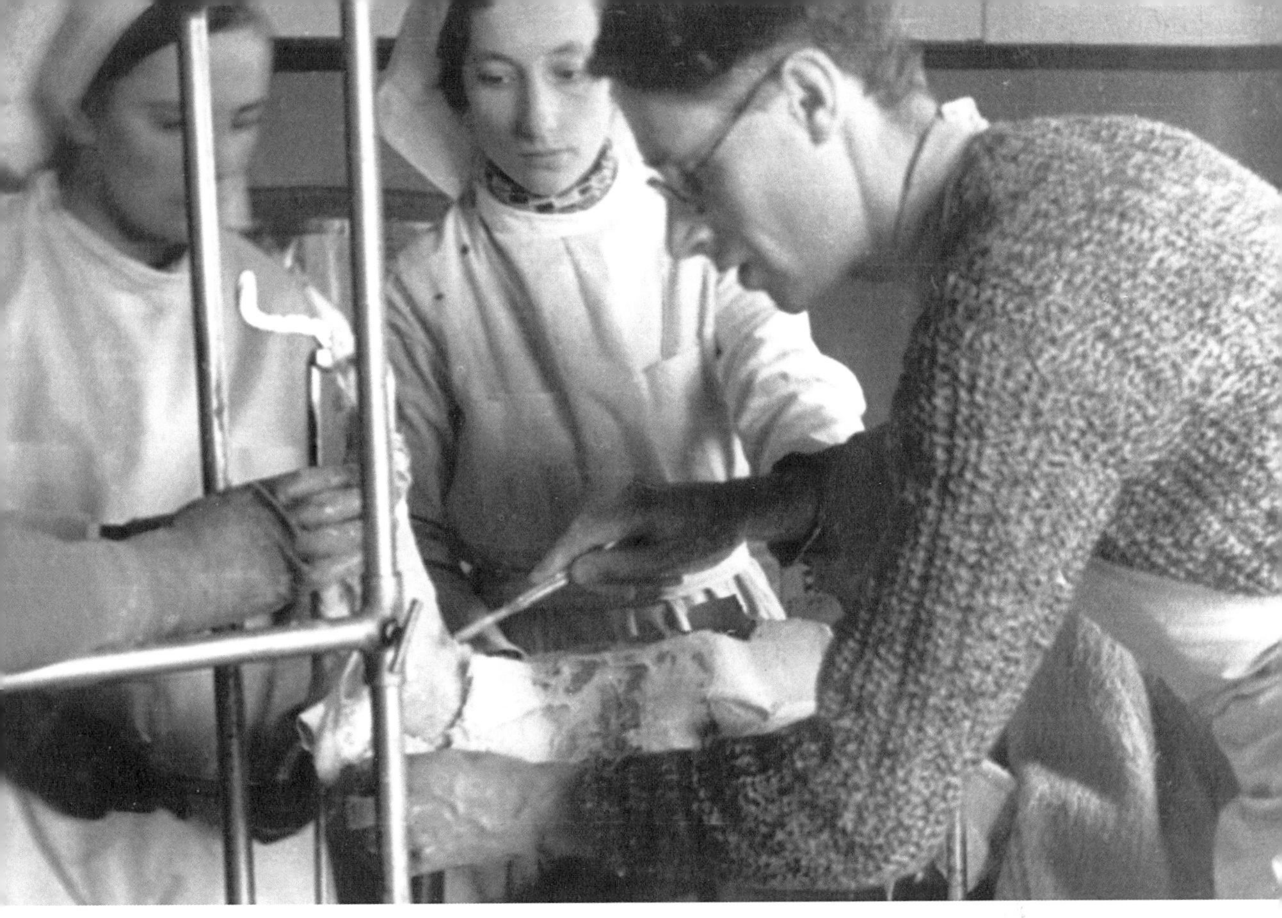

Cave hospital at La Bisbal de Falset. MARX MEMORIAL LIBRARY

As the fronts moved, British medical staff worked in many different locations. During the Battle of the Ebro in 1938, a large cave (above) was chosen as the site for a provisional hospital to protect the wounded from bombardment by enemy aviation. Prisoners and civilians, like this young boy (opposite, above), who was badly injured during a bombing raid, were also given treatment.

Aurora Fernández was one of the young Spanish women trained by British nurses to help with the wounded.

MARX MEMORIAL LIBRARY

The British doctor, Reggie Saxton, saved many lives through his work with a mobile transfusion unit. He was amongst the doctors using and developing revolutionary new techniques for the transfusion of preserved blood, which were widely used during the war in Spain and saved countless lives.

Dr Reggie Saxton giving a transfusion in the cave hospital.

MARX MEMORIAL LIBRARY

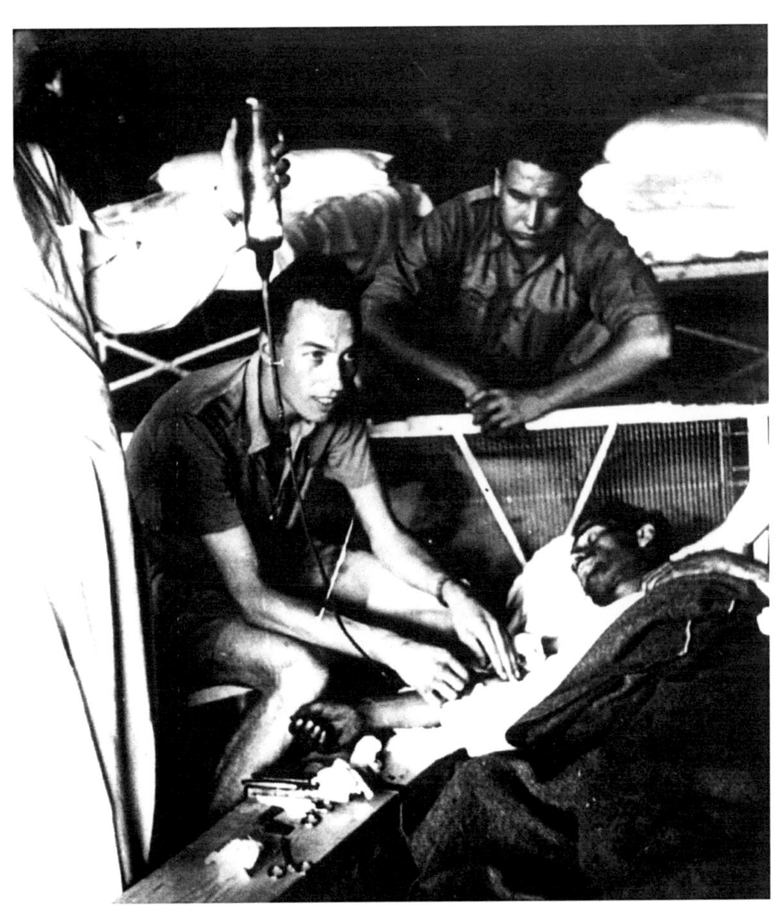

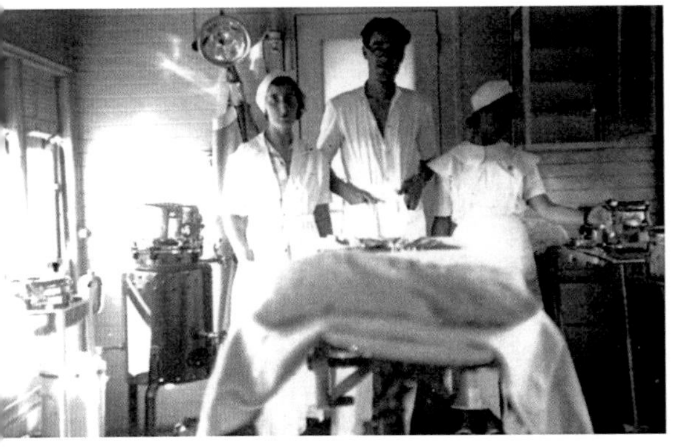

Scottish nurse Ann Murray in the operating theatre of a train.

MARX MEMORIAL LIBRARY

Hospital train evacuating the wounded.

MARX MEMORIAL LIBRARY

Railway tunnels were sometimes used as temporary hospitals. Scottish nurse Ann Murray worked in one of the train carriages converted for use as an operating theatre. To protect the casualties from enemy bombardment, the train would remain in a tunnel till the wounded could be transferred to an evacuation train stationed alongside for transport to the rearguard hospitals.

Most foreign medical workers were withdrawn from Spain together with the International Brigades in September 1938. However, several British nurses crossed over the border with the thousands of refugees fleeing Franco. They continued their work under the horrendous conditions that prevailed in the camps in France (see opposite), where civilians and the remnants of the Republican army were herded together and fenced in on beaches with no shelter or medical supplies.

MARGARET POWELL
was one of the volunteer nurses who helped in the refugee camps. The Republican government in exile awarded her the title of "Dame of the Order of Loyalty to the Spanish Republic" in recognition of her "valiant action as a nurse" and her "self sacrifice and devotion to our wounded and to our war victims".

Margaret Powell receiving her award from the Republican government in exile, with Luis Portillo (left) and Welsh Brigader Jim Brewer.

Camp for Spanish refugees in France, 1939.

BENICASIM

Here for a little we pause.
The air is heavy with sun and salt and colour.
On palm and lemon-tree, on cactus and oleander
a dust of dust and salt and pollen lies.
And the bright villas
sit in a row like perched macaws,
and rigid and immediate yonder
the mountains rise.

And it seems to me we have come
into a bright-painted landscape of Acheron.
For along the strand
in bleached cotton pyjamas, on rope-soled tread,
wander the risen-from-the-dead,
the wounded, the maimed, the halt.
Or they lay bare their hazarded flesh to the salt
air, the recaptured sun,
or bathe in the tideless sea, or sit fingering the sand.

But narrow is this place, narrow is this space
of garlanded sun and leisure and colour, of return
to life and release from living. Turn
(Turn not!) sight inland:
there, rigid as death and unforgiving, stand
the mountains – and close at hand.

Sylvia Townsend Warner,
a British writer and poet, wrote this poem after
visiting a convalescent hospital where many
International Brigaders recovered from their wounds.

Antifascistas

Art for the Cause

Drawing of a militiawoman by Felicia Browne.

LAWRENCE & WISHART

THE VOLUNTEER

Tell them in England, if they ask
What brought us to these wars,
To this plateau beneath the night's
Grave manifold of stars –

It was not fraud or foolishness,
Glory, revenge, or pay:
We came because our open eyes
*Could see no other way.**

There was no other way to keep
Man's flickering truth alight:
These stars will witness that our course
Burned briefer, not less bright.

Beyond the wasted olive-groves,
The furthest lift of land,
There calls a country that was ours
And here shall be regained.

Shine on us, memoried and real,
Green-water-silken meads:
Rivers of home, refresh our path
Whom here your influence leads.

Here in a parched and stranger place
We fight for England free,
The good our fathers won for her,
The land they hoped to see.

Cecil Day Lewis,
later to become the Poet Laureate, wrote this tribute
to the International Brigades in 1938.

* "Their open eyes could see no other way" is inscribed
on the International Brigade Memorial in London's Jubilee Gardens.

Poets Stephen Spender, George Green (fourth and fifth from left) and Ewart Milne (left) with other volunteer ambulance drivers on their way to Spain. MARX MEMORIAL LIBRARY

THE INTERNATIONAL BRIGADES and the Spanish Civil War live on in literature, films, music and art. The war was notable for the way that many poets, writers and artists in Spain, Britain and around the world passionately supported the cause of the Spanish Republic. Several writers and poets, such as WH Auden, Stephen Spender and Sylvia Townsend Warner, went to Spain during the civil war to support the Republic; others took up arms to fight fascism and joined the International Brigades.

Antifascistas

MUSEO NACIONAL CENTRO DE ARTE REINA SOFÍA

The most famous work of art to come out of the Spanish Civil War is Pablo Picasso's masterpiece, "Guernica" (above). Painted in response to the terror bombing of the civilian population of Guernica by Franco's German and Italian allies in April 1937, it was displayed in the Spanish Republic's pavilion at the 1937 World's Fair in Paris.

The recruiting office of the International Brigades was based in the French capital, so many International Brigade volunteers visited the pavilion before travelling south to Spain. They saw Picasso's painting, along with works by other Spanish artists, including Joan Miró – who produced this striking image of an upraised arm and clenched fist (right) as a design for a stamp – and a film scripted by Luis Buñuel about the defence of Madrid.

AIDEZ
1FR
L'
ESPAGNE
Dans la lutte actuelle, je vois du côté fasciste les forces
périmées, de l'autre côté le peuple dont les immenses ressources
créatrices donneront à l'Espagne un élan qui étonnera
le monde.
Miró.

DACS

Artists Nan Youngman and Priscilla Thornycroft paint a hoarding in central London in February 1939.

Labour leader Clement Attlee (centre) at the Whitechapel Gallery in London with Brigaders Sol Frankel (left) and Clive Branson. "Guernica" was shown at the gallery in January 1939 for a fund-raising exhibition organised by the East London Aid Spain Committee.

The Battersea-based artist and poet Clive Branson, who studied at the Slade School of Fine Art in London, sketched these fellow International Brigade captives at a prisoner-of-war camp in Palencia. He was captured by Italian troops at Calaceite in March 1938. He was subsequently killed in action in Burma in 1944 during the Second World War.

ROSA BRANSON

Antifascistas

e of the artists who went to Spain was Felicia
wne, who had been at the Slade School of Fine
with Clive Branson and who sketched the
nish Republican militiamen opposite.
: joined a militia group and was killed near
dienta in Aragon in late August 1936,
oming the first British casualty of the war.

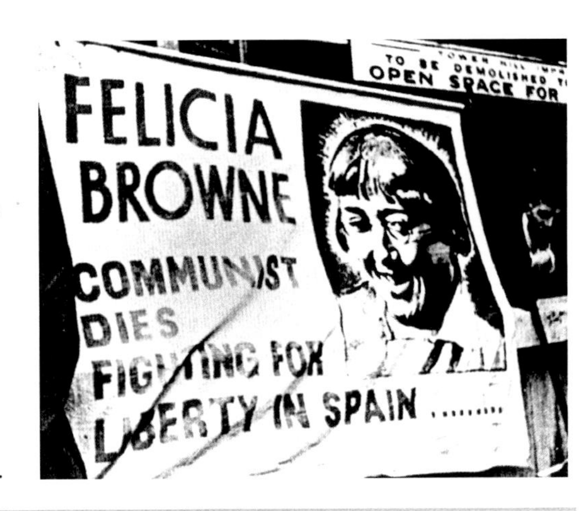

Poster for Felicia Browne exhibition.

Though he never joined the International Brigades, George Orwell (left) spent six months with the militia of the POUM revolutionary communist party, along with a small number of other British volunteers. He returned home to write "Homage to Catalonia", a memoir of his time in Spain, including his eye-witness account of how the revolutionary militias fell out with the Republican authorities in Barcelona in May 1937. The book later inspired Ken Loach's controversial film "Land and Freedom" (1995).

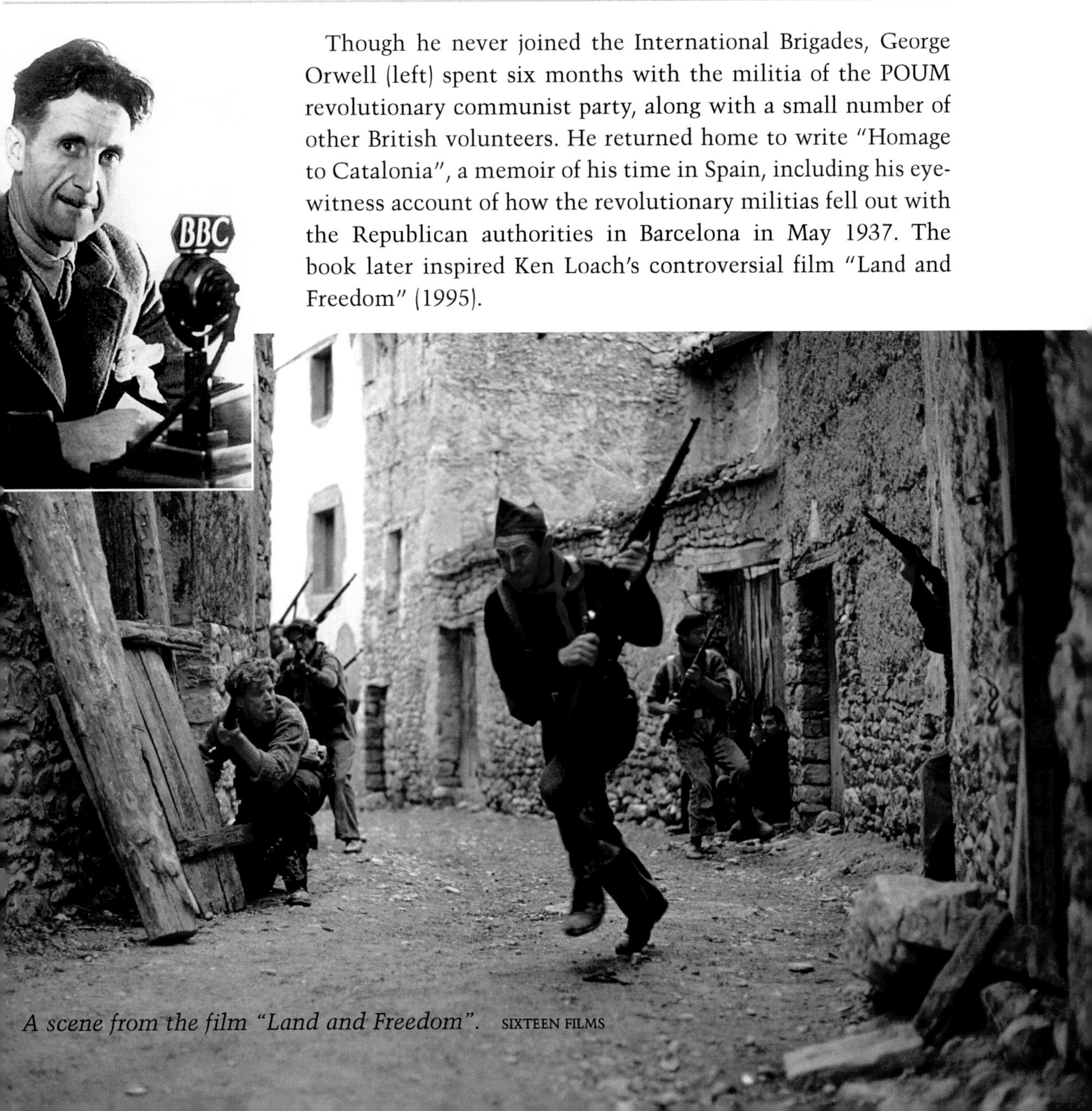

A scene from the film "Land and Freedom". SIXTEEN FILMS

A LETTER FROM ARAGON

John Cornford

This is a quiet sector of a quiet front.

We buried Ruiz in a new pine coffin,
But the shroud was too small and his washed feet stuck out,
The stink of his corpse came through the clean pine boards
And some of the bearers wrapped handkerchiefs round their faces. Death was not dignified
We hacked a ragged grave in the unfriendly earth
And fired a ragged volley over the grave.

You could tell from our listlessness, no one much missed him.

This is a quiet sector of a quiet front.
There is no poison gas and no H.E. *

But when they shelled the other end of the village
And the streets were choked with dust
Women came screaming out of the crumbling houses,
Clutched under one arm the naked rump of an infant.
I thought: how ugly fear is.

This is a quiet sector of a quiet front.
Our nerves are steady; we also sleep soundly.

In the clean hospital bed my eyes were so heavy
Sleep easily blotted out one ugly picture,
A wounded militiaman moaning on a stretcher,
Now out of danger, but still crying for water,
Strong against death, but unprepared for such pain.

This on a quiet front.

But when I shook hands to leave, an Anarchist worker
Said: 'Tell the workers of England
This was a war not of our own making.
We did not seek it.
But if ever the Fascists again rule Barcelona
It will be as a heap of ruins with us workers beneath it.'

• High explosive

Laurie Lee KATHY LEE

Another gifted young writer who wrote about his experiences in Spain was Laurie Lee, who joined the International Brigades for a few weeks in 1937 before being medically discharged on grounds of epilepsy. He had been living in Spain when the war broke out, which he vividly describes in his autobiographical "As I Walked Out One Midsummer Morning" (1969). In 1991 he published "A Moment of War", a memoir loosely based on his brief war service.

Several writers were killed in Spain while serving with the International Brigades. They included the poet Julian Bell (nephew of Virginia Woolf), who died driving an ambulance at the Battle of Brunete in July 1937. Christopher Caudwell was the author of several detective novels under his real name of Christopher St John Sprigg; he was killed at the Battle of Jarama in February 1937. The brilliant young poet John Cornford died in fighting near Córdoba in December 1936, along with the Marxist writer and literary critic Ralph Fox.

John Cornford

Christopher Caudwell

The poet Miles Tomalin (left), who served in the British Anti-Tank Battery, is pictured here in Spain with Humphrey (Hugh) Slater. Slater was another Slade School of Fine Art graduate and worked as a journalist before joining the International Brigades. After the war he wrote books on military tactics and novels inspired by his political activism and experiences in Spain, including "The Heretics" and "Conspirator", which was made into a Hollywood film in 1949.

MARX MEMORIAL LIBRARY

Benjamin Britten

WH Auden

Randall Swingler

The composer Benjamin Britten put music to words by poets WH Auden and Randall Swingler for his requiem "Ballad of Heroes" in tribute to fallen International Brigaders. Auden's lines end with the incantation to "Honour, honour them all", while Swingler's chorus declares:

"To you we speak, you numberless Englishmen,

To remind you of the greatness still among you

Created by these men who go from your towns

To fight for peace, for liberty and for you."

"Ballad of Heroes" received its first performance at the Queen's Hall, London, on 5 April 1939, when the London Symphony Orchestra was joined by 300 voices from Co-operative and Labour choirs. The concert was attended by International Brigaders carrying banners of the British Battalion.

HOMENAJE
DE DESPEDIDA
A LAS BRIGADAS INTERNACIONALES

Palabras de ANTONIO MACHADO; Versos de RAFAEL ALBERTI, MANUEL ALTOLAGUIRRE, PEDRO GARFIAS, JUAN GIL-ALBERT, MIGUEL HERNÁNDEZ, JOSÉ HERRERA PETERE, PABLO NERUDA, JUAN PAREDES, PÉREZ INFANTE, EMILIO PRADOS, ARTURO SERRANO PLAJA y LORENZO VARELA

EDICIONES ESPAÑOLAS

Commemorative book published in 1938 to mark the departure of the International Brigades from Spain.

Withdrawal of the British Battalion

The final military parade of the British Battalion photographed by Robert Capa. Welsh Brigader Alun Menai Williams bears the British Battalion banner and Jim Brewer the Republican flag.

ROBERT CAPA/MAGNUM PHOTOS

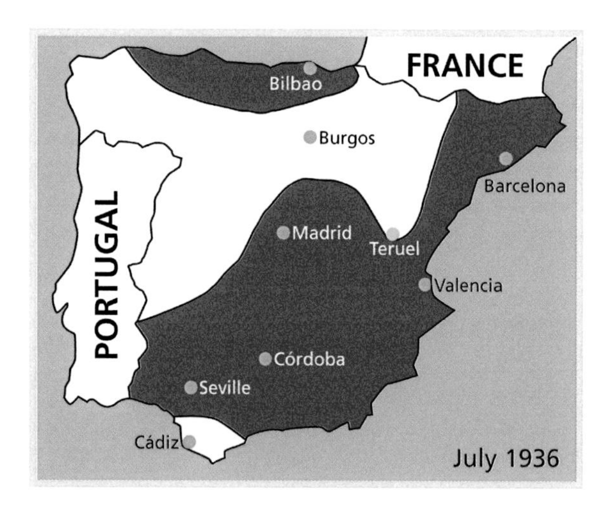

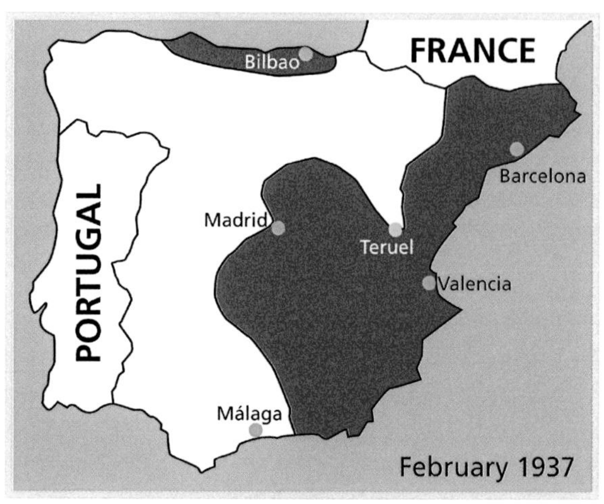

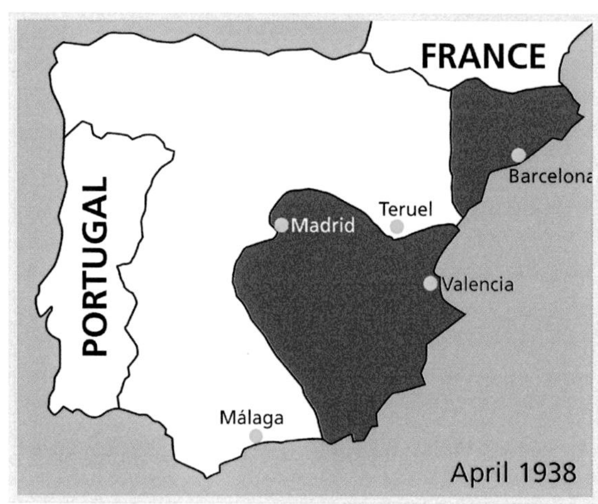

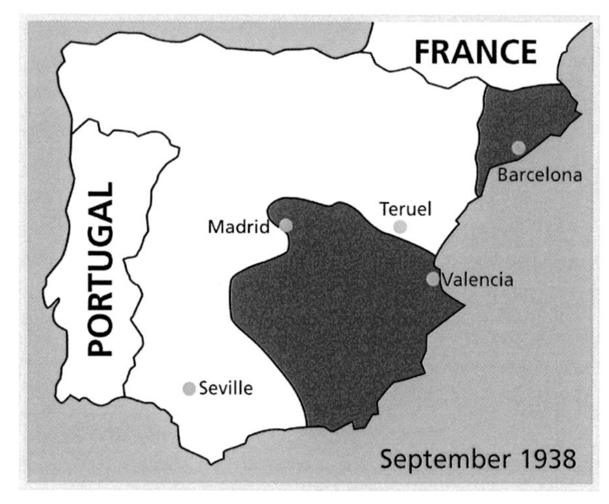

PROGRESS OF THE WAR

Despite heroic defensive efforts by the Republicans, the Nationalists' military superiority, backed by the forces of Hitler and Mussolini, eventually told.

 *Republican-held Spain* 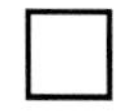 *Nationalist-held Spain*

Survivors of the British Battalion at Marçà, 23 September 1938.

MARX MEMORIAL LIBRARY

ON 21 SEPTEMBER 1938, Juan Negrín, the Spanish premier, announced the Republic's intention to repatriate all foreign volunteers in a vain attempt to secure help from Britain and France to mediate a peace with Franco. But on 23 September, during the Battle of the Ebro, the British Battalion was called upon one last time. After sustaining an immense five-hour artillery barrage at Sierra de Lavall de la Torre, the men of the battalion were caught in murderous rebel cross-fire. Nevertheless, they remained in their positions right up until the trenches were overrun. When the battalion was withdrawn on that same evening, the losses of the previous three days were realised: over 200 members of the battalion were killed, wounded or missing. It was a tragic and heartbreaking end to their role in Spain.

Antifascistas

The depleted ranks of British volunteers did not leave Spain immediately. On 16 October 1938 all the foreign volunteers in the 35th Division were paraded and reviewed, and several of their number received promotions and commendations.

The final appearance of the battalion was at a farewell parade in Barcelona at the end of October 1938, at which important Republican figures, including President Manuel Azaña and Prime Minister Negrín, expressed their thanks to the Internationals. The speech by Dolores Ibárruri (below), the communist member of parliament from Asturias forever known as La Pasionaria, delivered to the more than 13,000 watching volunteers, was the highlight of an extremely emotional occasion:

"Comrades of the International Brigades! Political reasons, reasons of state, the good of that same cause for which you offered your blood with limitless generosity, send some of you back to your countries and some to forced exile. You can go with pride. You are history. You are legend. You are the heroic example of the solidarity and the universality of democracy... We will not forget you; and, when the olive tree of peace puts forth its leaves, entwined with the laurels of the Spanish Republic's victory, come back!"

The final parade in Barcelona on 28 October 1938. MARX MEMORIAL LIBRARY

Carnet presented to departing Brigaders.

The Anti-Fascist Fight Continues

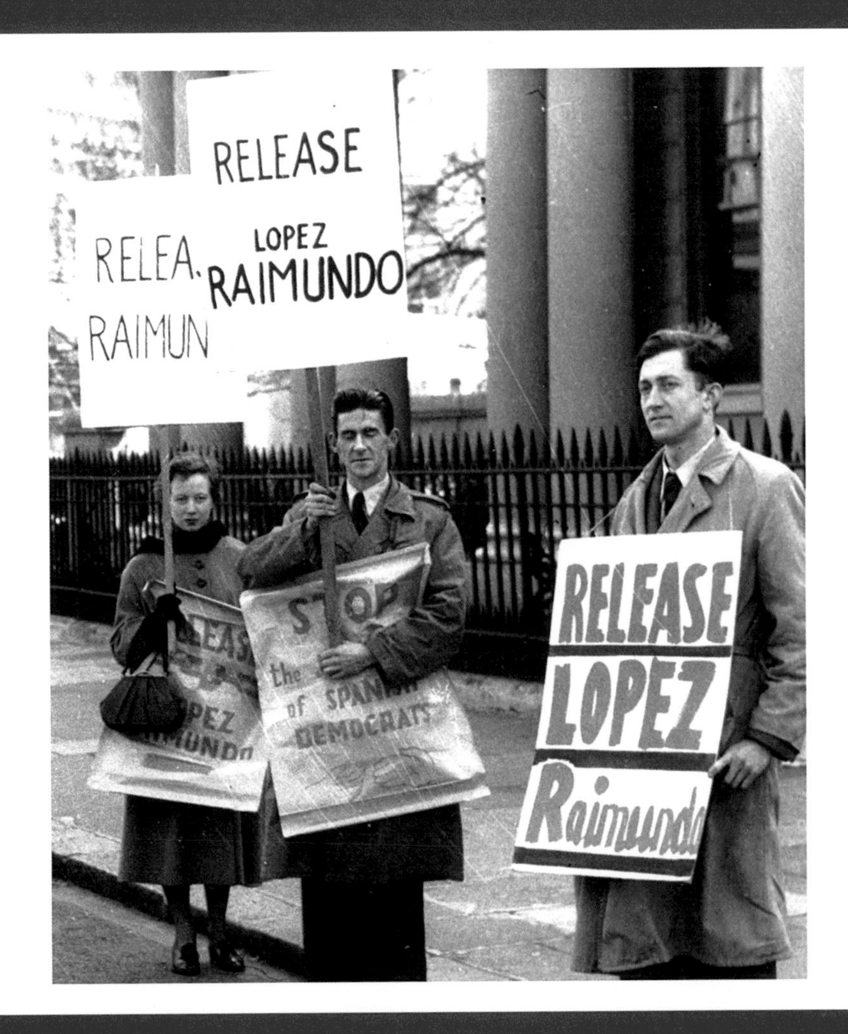

Alex Digges (centre), secretary of the International Brigade Association, with protesters outside the Spanish embassy in London in 1952.

SID KAUFMAN

British and Irish prisoners cross the frontier at Irún into France. MARX MEMORIAL LIBRARY

The British Battalion arrives at Newhaven. MARX MEMORIAL LIBRARY

MOST BRITISH VOLUNTEERS returned home in December 1938 but some prisoners remained in Franco's jails until March 1940. Back in Britain, the Brigaders continued to campaign to change the policy of the British government towards the Spanish Republic and spoke at meetings to raise funds for medical supplies. They formed the International Brigade Association (IBA) in March 1939.

Franco, pictured above with Hitler, declared victory on 1 April 1939 after his troops had marched into Madrid. Exhausted and abandoned, the Spanish Republic had finally collapsed after two-and-a-half years of resistance. But the fight against fascism in Spain and the rest of Europe had not ended. As the International Brigaders had predicted, a world war would soon follow Franco's victory in Spain. When Hitler invaded Poland on 1 September 1939, five months after the end of the Spanish Civil War, Britain and France finally ended their disastrous policy of appeasing Hitler and declared war on Germany.

Stalin's signing of a non-aggression pact between the Soviet Union and Germany in August 1939 came as a shock to the Spanish veterans, though the outbreak of the Second World War the following month initially appeared to offer the opportunity to continue the fight against fascism started in Spain. Veterans began to enlist in the armed forces, but the IBA, in line with the Communist Party, quickly declared its opposition to the conflict, arguing it was an imperialist, not an anti-fascist war. Still bitter at what they saw as the British government's betrayal of the Spanish Republic, many Brigaders followed suit. Communist opposition to the war was only dropped following the Nazi invasion of the Soviet Union in June 1941.

Despite the IBA's initial opposition to the war and the attitude of the British government, which was extremely wary of accepting veterans from Spain into the British armed forces, a number of Brigaders served with distinction in the Second World War.

Tom Wintringham, the former British Battalion commander at the Battle of Jarama, was the driving force behind the creation in 1940 of the Home Guard, a militia unit that would fight the Germans if their forces landed in Britain.

Another battalion commander, Bill Alexander, graduated top of his intake at Sandhurst and served as a captain in the British Army's Reconnaissance Corps in Italy, France and Germany.

Len Crome, the former commander of the medical services of the 35th Division in Spain, was drafted into the British Army as a captain in the Royal Army Medical Corps. In the battles around Monte Cassino in Italy in 1944, Crome won the Military Cross for showing extraordinary bravery by carrying on working despite heavy enemy fire.

During the Second World War many thousands of Spanish Republicans fought with the Allies and in the French Resistance. Spain remained officially neutral, but Franco wanted the Axis powers to triumph and sent some 50,000 troops to fight alongside Hitler's army against the Soviet Union. Following the defeat of Hitler and Mussolini, International Brigade veterans hoped that the victorious Allies would topple Franco's regime. It was not to be. After the Cold War broke out between the United States and the Soviet Union in the late 1940s, Franco became an anti-communist ally of the US and his dictatorship lasted until his death on 20 November 1975.

Some 400,000 Spaniards lost their lives in the Spanish Civil War. The same number fled into exile and up to a million were

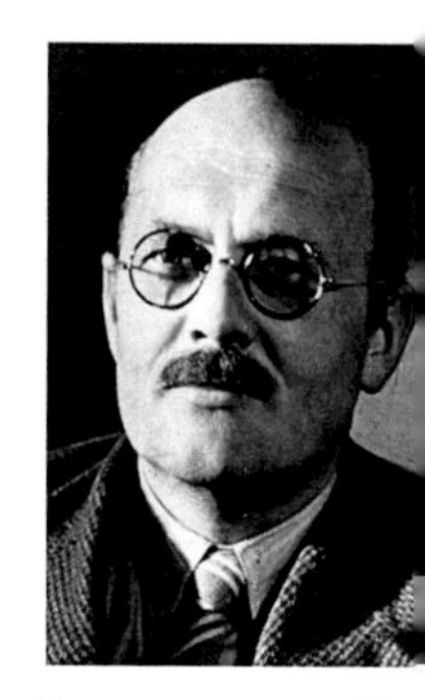

Tom Wintringha

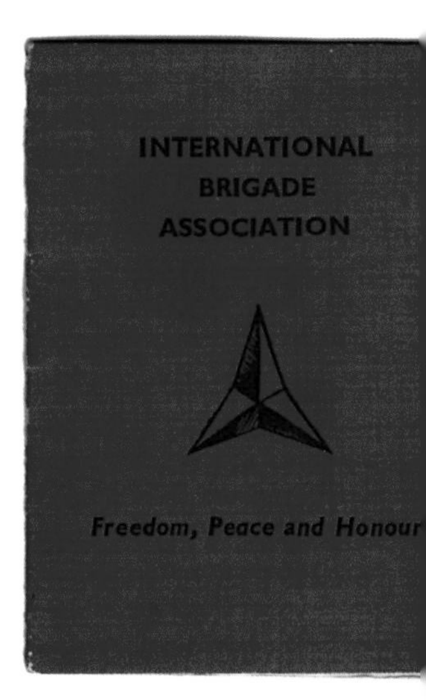

IBA membership car

Bill Alexander MARX MEMORIAL LIBRARY

Len Crome

Spanish Republican prisoners greet US troops liberating the Nazi concentration camp at Mauthausen in May 1945.

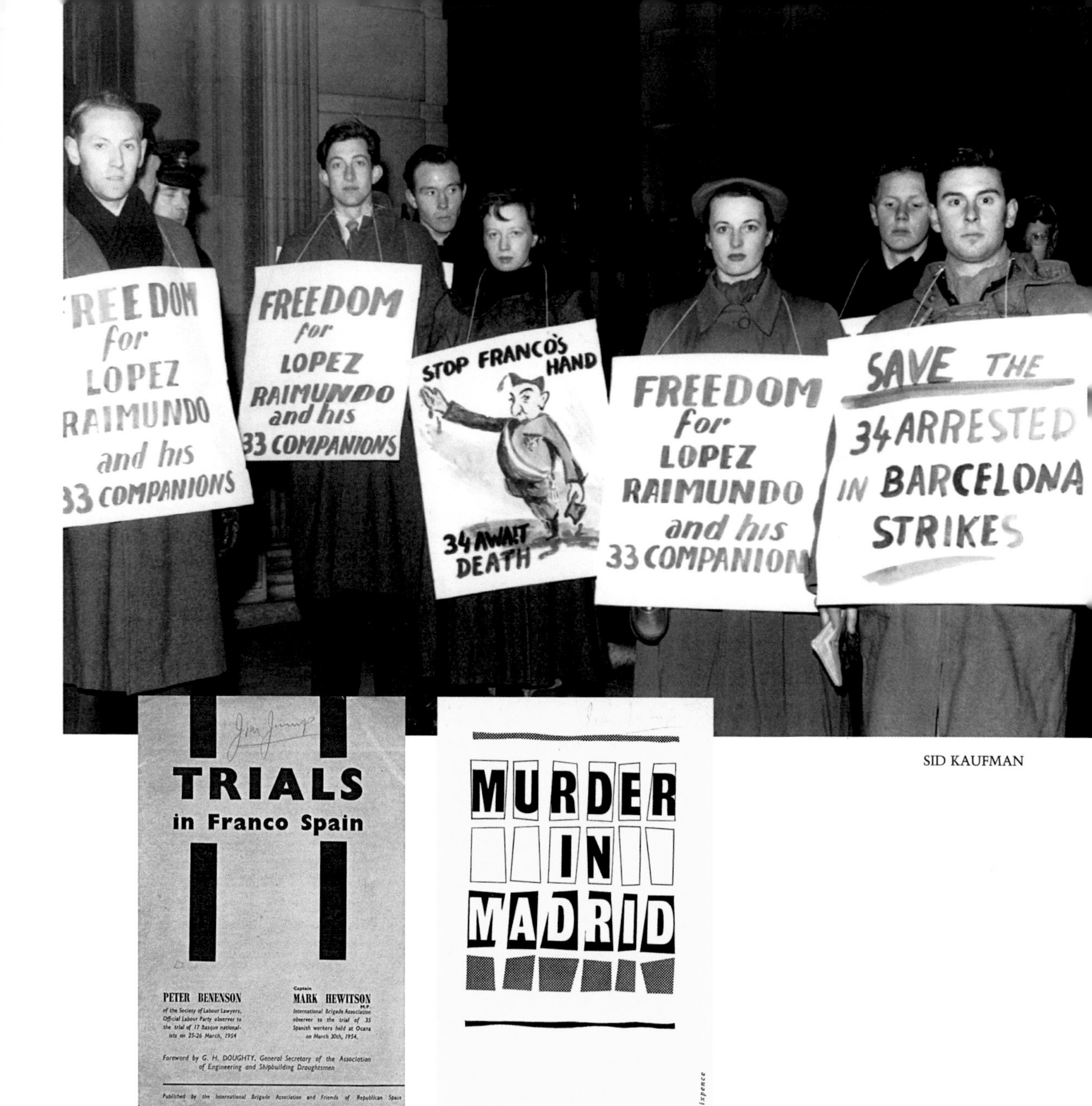

SID KAUFMAN

thrown into jail by Franco. The dictatorship continued to imprison, torture and execute its opponents until its dying days. In Britain, the IBA campaigned to help Spain's political prisoners, sending food parcels to their families and paying for British lawyers and MPs to attend their trials.

Antifascistas

Remembering the Volunteers

The International Brigade memorial in Glasgow beside the Clyde.

Brochure produced in 1984 to raise funds for a national memorial to the volunteers from the British Isles.

INTERNATIONAL BRIGADE MEMORIAL APPEAL

Sponsors: Isabel Brown
James Cameron
Moss Evans
Michael Foot M.P.
Lord Elwyn-Jones
Ivor Montagu
Arthur Scargill
Sogat 82, William Keys
Dame Janet Vaughan
Lord Willis

Nearly fifty years have passed since more than 2,000 men and went from Britain to Spain to serve as soldiers, doctors, nurse ambulance drivers in the International Brigades. More than a them died defending the Spanish government and democrac Franco and the other rebel generals who were backed by arm troops sent by the dictators Hitler and Mussolini.

These volunteers went because they understood that fasc racial and political persecution and the destruction of freedo knew that every advance of fascism increased the danger tha homes and families would be threatened by war.

They came from all walks of life — they went to fight bec the words of the poet C. Day Lewis "they could see no other Despite hardship and danger, they played their part in every the three-year-long war in Spain.

These men and women saved the honour of Britain at a ti Hitler and Mussolini were being helped and appeased by the government of the day. They alerted the British people and g time to prepare for victory over fascism in the world war.

In 1986 the world will commemorate the 50th anniversary outbreak of the Spanish War. The International Brigade Memo has been launched to provide a permanent memorial in a pub London to honour the volunteers from Britain, so that their v sacrifice will be a reminder and an inspiration.

We ask for your generous financial support to make this p success.

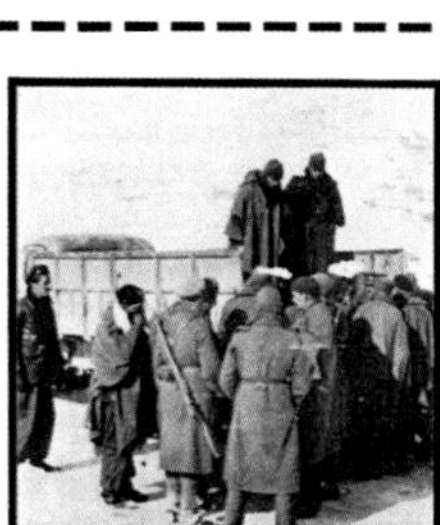

The 'grub' arrives for the Britis the snow at Teruel.

PLEASE POST THIS

To: Chris Birch, Treasurer, 1 London SW6 4QB.
In support of the Internatio enclose our donation.

Name ____________

Address (to which receipt wi ____________

____

Organisation ____________

Amount enclosed £ ____________

1936 1939

Top Right — British nurses in the operating room on a hospital train, Catalonia, 1938.

Centre — A group of British volunteers, Brunete, 1937.

Top Left — The Major Attlee Company of the British Battalion.

INTERNATIONAL BRIGADE MEMORIAL APPEAL

GLC assisted

Unveiling of the International Brigade memorial in London's Jubilee Gardens on 5 October 1985 by former Labour Party leader Michael Foot (on right of the memorial).

International Brigade veterans parade the British Battalion banner through Barcelona in 1988 to commemorate the 50th anniversary of the departure of the volunteers from the city.

ANDREW WIARD

DESPITE ALL FRANCO'S EFFORTS to the contrary, democracy was restored to Spain after his death and free elections were held in 1977 for the first time since 1936. When they returned, Brigaders were enthusiastically welcomed by the Spanish people.

In 2007, the Spanish parliament passed a law conferring Spanish citizenship on the surviving volunteers. This finally fulfilled the promise made by the Republican government in October 1938.

The Spanish poet Rafael Alberti, who was a member of the famous "Generation of '27" group of writers and artists before the Spanish Civil War, presented this sketch to all the veterans who attended a 60th anniversary reunion in Madrid in 1996. The dedication says: "This dove of peace for the valiant International Brigades".

Veterans receiving their Spanish citizenship at a ceremony held in the Spanish embassy in London on 9 June 2009; from left: Thomas Watters, Lou Kenton, Joseph Kahn, Sam Lesser, Penny Feiwel, Jack Edwards and Paddy Cochrane. GRAEME ROBERTSON/THE GUARDIAN

"Your efforts were not in vain.
Your ideals are part of the foundations
of our democracy in Spain today."

– Carles Casajuana,
the Spanish Ambassador in London, addressing
International Brigade veterans when granting them
Spanish citizenship.

Memorials to the International Brigades, clockwise from top left, in London, Belfast, Cardiff, Manchester, and Morata de Tajuña on the Jarama battlefield.

There are memorials to the International Brigades in all the major cities and in many towns and villages across Britain and Ireland. In July each year, hundreds of people gather in London's Jubilee Gardens in front of the national memorial – created by sculptor Ian Walters – to pay tribute to the volunteers who left from the British Isles. There are also several memorials to the International Brigades in Spain.

The International Brigade Association donated its archives to the Marx Memorial Library in London in 1975. The collection, known as the International Brigade Memorial Archive, is consulted by students, researchers and historians from around the world. The main banner of the British Battalion hangs in the library's hall and a vast array of surviving official documents from the British Brigaders – ranging from battle orders to the work of the dependancy committees and ambulance drivers – is preserved there.

Other archives are held across the UK and Ireland, in particular the extensive collection of interviews with Brigaders at the Imperial War Museum, London, and the Spanish Civil War archive at the Working Class Movement Library in Salford.

INTERNATIONAL BRIGADE MEMORIAL TRUST

Veterans of the International Brigade Association joined together with families, friends, supporters and historians to form the International Brigade Memorial Trust (IBMT) in 2001. The Trust keeps alive the memory and spirit of the men and women who volunteered to fight alongside the Spanish people to defend democracy during the civil war of 1936–39.
The IBMT:

- Helps maintain the memorials to the International Brigades in the British Isles and Spain and supports local initiatives for new ones.
- Publishes a regular newsletter
- Has a comprehensive website:
  www.international-brigades.org.uk
- Develops links with sister organisations throughout the world
- Organises educational projects, lectures and exhibitions
- Supports researchers in providing information on the history of the British Battalion and individual volunteers
- Holds commemorative events

Contact the Trust at: secretary@international-brigades.org.uk

The IBMT banner is a replica of the banner presented to the British Battalion by the Artists International Association.

British volunteers before the Battle of the Ebro. MARX MEMORIAL LIBRARY

'You are legend...'

Why is it important to remember the International Brigade volunteers today?

- *The Spanish Civil War, in which the International Brigaders participated, is regarded by historians as a prelude to the Second World War, the most important conflict of the 20th century.*

- *The volunteers who went from the British Isles and other countries set an unprecedented example of international solidarity.*

- *They fought against fascism and on the side of a democratically elected government that stood for social justice in areas such as health and education, for new rights for women, for free trade unions and for respect towards differing national identities. These are values that endure today.*

- *The volunteers who went to Spain were an exceptional group of individuals. Several of them afterwards became great soldiers, leading trade union and political figures and well-known writers and poets.*

- *The courage and self-sacrifice of the International Brigades in Spain continue to be an inspiration to people around the world.*

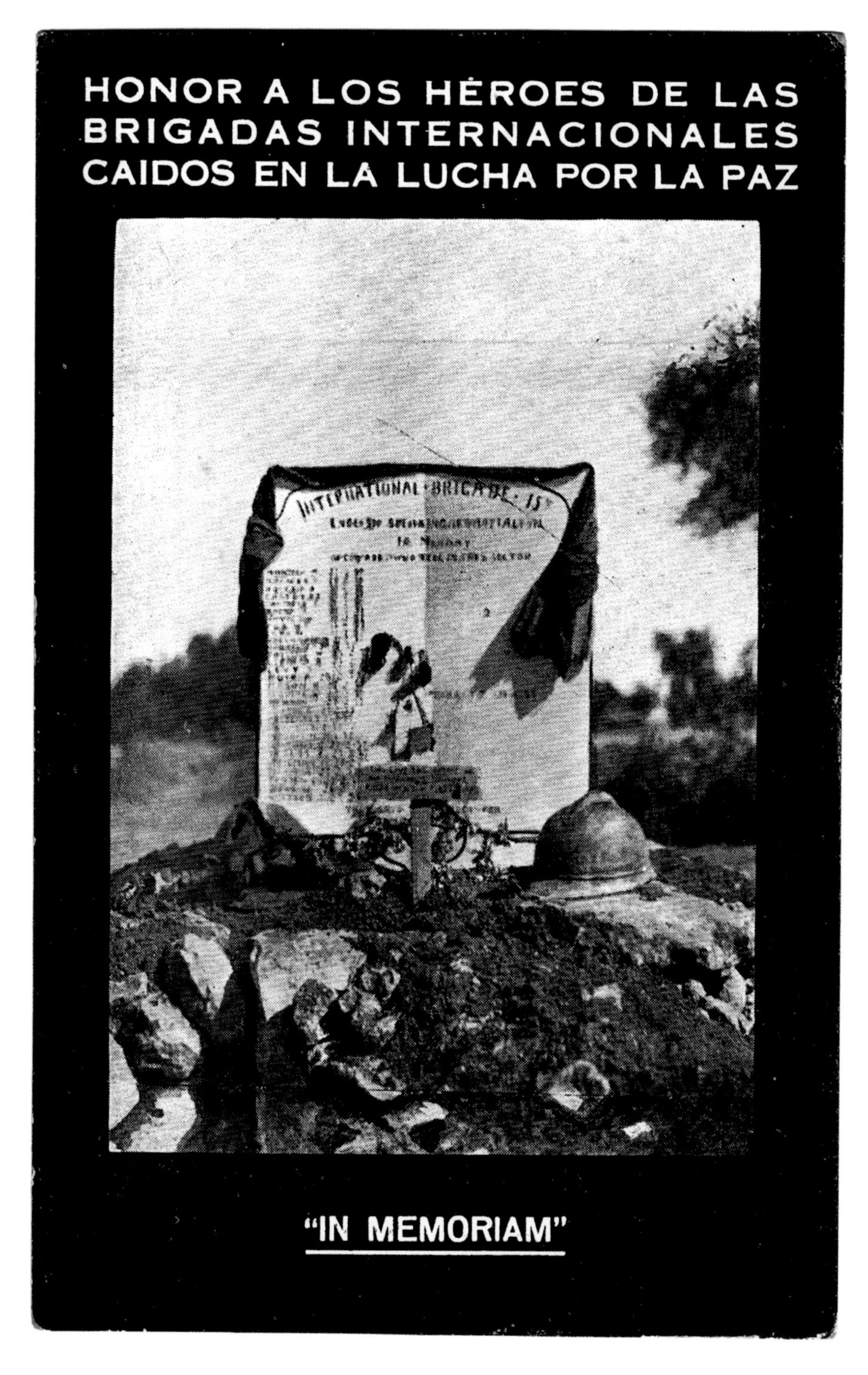

Postcard published by the International Brigades Commissariat showing the gravestone for the dead of the XV International Brigade, including the British Battalion, at Jarama. The memorial and graves were destroyed after the war.

Died in Spain

This list of those who died in Spain – or shortly afterwards as a result of their time in Spain – comprises details of volunteers from Britain and Ireland, together with those from other nationalities who fought in the British Battalion and Anti-Tank Battery. As a rule, the "Where from" column gives the last residence before departure to Spain, though this might have been a "care of" or relative's address or a place of work. Whilst every effort has been made to ensure the list is as accurate as possible, it is constantly being revised as new information becomes available and will inevitably contain some errors, oversights and omissions.

Surname	First name(s)	Where from	Date	Place of death
Aaronberg	Maurice	Leeds	February 1937	Jarama
Abramson	Nathan	London	April 1938	Gandesa
Addley	Harry	Folkestone	December 1936	Boadilla
Airlie	Frank	Bellshill	30 July 1938	Gandesa
Alexander	John	Dundee	July 1937	Brunete
Allstop	Geoffrey L	Rotherham/Canada	1 March 1938	Caspe
Alwyn	James	Bolton	February 1937	Jarama
Anastasiou	Antonis	London/Cyprus	March 1938	Caspe
Armstrong	Alexander	Manchester	February 1937	Jarama
Ash	Francis	Glasgow	March 1938	Aragon
Atkinson	Jack	Hull	21 February 1937	Jarama
Avgherinos	Constantinos	London/Cyprus	April 1937	In hospital from wounds sustained at Jarama
Avner	Sidney	London	December 1936	Boadilla
Bailey	William	Haywood	June 1937	In hospital from pneumonia
Ball	William H	Reading	22 February 1937	In hospital from wounds sustained at Jarama
Banks	William	Manchester	March 1938	Aragon
Barry	Jack William	Australia	December 1936	Boadilla
Batson	Percy	Canada	7 February 1938	In Benicasim hospital from wounds sustained at Teruel
Baxter	Norman	Leeds	February 1937	Jarama
Beadles	Richard	Birkenhead	February 1937	Jarama
Beales	William Thomas George	Isle of Wight	March 1938	Aragon

Antifascistas

Beaton	John William	Glasgow	March 1938	Aragon
Beattie	William	Belfast	23 July 1937	Brunete
Beckett	Clement	Oldham	12 February 1937	Jarama
Beckett	William Benjamin	London	March 1938	Aragon
Bell	Julian	London	17 July 1937	Brunete
Bennett	Gordon Alexander	Birmingham	July 1938	Gandesa
Bentley	James	Hull	31 March 1938	Calaceite
Berry	John	Edinburgh	12 February 1937	Jarama
Bibby	Leonard W	London	15 February 1937	Jarama
Birch	Lorimer G	London	20 December 1936	Boadilla
Bird	Richard A	London	July 1937	Brunete
Black	John Donald	Dover	11 July 1937	Brunete
Black	John G	Glasgow	February 1937?	Jarama
Blair	Robert Cooper	London	April 1938	Gandesa
Bogle	William John	Liverpool	February 1937	Jarama
Bolger	Bernard Ray	London	8 April 1937	Jarama
Bonar	Hugh	Co. Donegal	April 1937	Jarama
Bond	Kenneth Purnell	Hayes, Kent	July 1938	Gandesa
Bonnar	Henry Andrew	Glasgow	December 1936	Chimorra
Bonner	Alex	Glasgow	27 February 1937	Jarama
Bosley	Harry Thomas	Stoke	July 1938	Gandesa
Boswell	Bruce J	Coventry	31 July 1938	Gandesa
Boyce	William George	Bristol	20 January 1938	Teruel
Boyle	Daniel	Belfast	September 1938	Sierra Caballs
Bradbury	Kenneth	Oldham	20 January 1938	Teruel
Brannan	Thomas	Blantyre	February 1937	Jarama
Breedon	Stuart Arthur	Edgware	31 July 1938	Gandesa
Brent	William	Barnsley	March 1938	Aragon
Bridges	Robert	Leith	27 February 1937	Jarama
Bright	George	Thornbury-on-Tees	12 February 1937	Jarama
Briskey	William	London	12 February 1937	Jarama
Broadbent	Clement	Dewsbury	9 September 1938	Gandesa
Bromley	Thomas	Southwick, Staffs	April 1938	Gandesa
Brookes	Harry Marcus	Ormeston	July 1938	Gandesa
Brookfield	Norman Ernest	Maidstone	September 1938	Sierra Caballs
Brown	Frank Arthur	Manchester	31 July 1938	Gandesa
Brown	George	Manchester	6 July 1937	Villanueva de la Cañada
Brown	William J	Newmilns	27 February 1937	Jarama
Brown	William Norman	Stockport	March 1938	Aragon
Browne	Felicia	London	28 August 1936	Aragon
Browne	Michael	London	March 1938	Aragon
Bruce	John Murray	Alexandria	13 February 1937	Executed whilst a prisoner at Jarama
Buffman	David	Leeds	September 1938	Sierra Caballs
Burke	Edward Henry	Oxford	12 February 1937	In Federal Hospital, Madrid, from wounds sustained at Lopera
Burke	Thomas	Glasgow	July 1937	Brunete
Burton	William J	Bristol	February 1937	Jarama
Byrom	Hugh	Manchester	March 1938	Aragon
Cameron	Donald	Glasgow	14 February 1937	Jarama
Campbell	John	Belfast	27 February 1937	Jarama
Campeau	G 'Ralph'	London	15 February 1937	In hospital from wounds sustained at Jarama

Canaris	Ahillea C	London/Cyprus	July 1937	Brunete
Cantorovitch	Ralph	Manchester	July 1937	Brunete
Caplan	Philip	London	13 February 1937	Jarama
Capps	Alfred Ernest	London	20 January 1938	Teruel
Carritt	Anthony	Oxford	July 1937	Brunete
Carter	Barton 'Nick'	London/USA	April 1938	Aragon
Carter	Thomas J	Hartlepool	27 February 1937	Jarama
Cassidy	James	Glasgow	February 1937	Jarama
Chambers	William	London	June 1937	Huesca
Charlton	Patrick	Leeds	February 1937	Jarama
Clasper	Walter	London	March 1938	Aragon
Clive	Lewis	London	1 August 1938	Hill 481, Gandesa
Coady	Dennis	Dublin	12 January 1937	Las Rozas
Cockburn	James	London/Dundee	12 January 1937	Las Rozas or Lopera
Codling	Stephen	South Shields	31 March 1938	Calaceite
Coles	William	Cardiff	February 1937	Jarama
Connolly	John	Glasgow	27 February 1937	Jarama
Conroy	Frank	Kildare	28 December 1936	Lopera
Constantinou	Christos	London/Cyprus	March 1938	Belchite
Conway	Chris 'Kit'	Dublin	12 February 1937	Jarama
Coombes	James E	London	September 1937	Belchite
Cormack	Charles E	London	August 1938	Gandesa
Cornford	John	Cambridge	28 December 1936	Lopera
Corry	George William	Cleckheaton	March 1938	Caspe
Coutts	Robert B	North Shields	14 January 1937	Las Rozas
Cox	Matthew	Dundee	March 1938	Caspe
Cox	Raymond Arthur	Southampton	December 1936	Boadilla
Cox	William H	London	February 1937	Jarama
Craig	Allan	Glasgow	22 February 1937	Jarama
Craig	George I	Ulmanston	February 1937	Jarama
Crawford	William J	Glasgow	28 February 1937	Jarama
Crispin	Walter Ernest	London	August 1938	Gandesa
Crombie	Fraser	Kirkcaldy	9 July 1937	Brunete
Cross	Edward Harold	London	April 1938	Gandesa
Cruikshank	Robert	Glasgow	April 1938	Gandesa
Cummings	Alec	Cardiff	September 1938	Sierra Caballs
Cunningham	James D	Glasgow	28 July 1938	Gandesa
Curley	Patrick	Alexandria	February 1937	Jarama
Dalglish	John	Leith	27 February 1937	Jarama
Daly	Peter	Enniscorthy	6 September 1937	In hospital from wounds sustained at Purburrel Hill, Quinto
Davidovitch	Maurice	London	12 February 1937	Jarama
Davidson	Thomas	Aberdeen	April 1938	Gandesa
Davie	Adam	Glasgow	27 February 1937	Jarama
Davies	Harold	Neath	14 February 1937	Jarama
Davies	William J	Tonypandy	July 1937	Brunete
Davis	William	Dublin	July 1937	Brunete
De Goode	George Marcel	London	July 1937	Brunete
Deegan	Vincent Leo	Brighton	March 1938	Aragon
Degan	George	Balloch	22 January 1938	In hospital from wounds sustained at Teruel
Dewar	Archibald	Aberdeen	17 March 1938	Calaceite
Dewhurst	Paul 'Francis'	London	July 1937	Brunete

Antifascistas

Dickenson	Edward Alfred	London	13 February 1937	Executed whilst a prisoner at Jarama
Dickson	William John	Prestonpans	July 1937	Brunete
Dobson	Harry	Rhondda	1 August 1938	In Falset hospital of wounds sustained at Hill 481, Gandesa
Dobson	Walter	Leeds	March 1938	Aragon
Docherty	Frank	Glasgow	July 1938	Gandesa
Dolan	John	Glasgow	27 February 1937	Jarama
Dolan	Thomas W	Sunderland	27 February 1937	Jarama
Dolling	Charles	London	July 1937	Brunete
Domegan	James C	Belfast	September 1937	Sierra Caballs
Donaldson	James	Fife	June 1938	Barcelona
Donaldson	William J	Glasgow	22 January 1938	Teruel
Donavan	Tom	Skibereen	March 1938	Aragon
Donnell	Stanley	Glasgow	April 1938	Calaceite
Donnelly	Charles	Dublin	27 February 1937	Jarama
Doran	Archibald Lester	Weston-super-Mare	13 February 1937	Jarama
Douglas	John	Glasgow	February 1937	Jarama
Dowsey	HA	Dover	February 1937	Jarama
Drinkwater	Freeman 'Frank'	Burnley	July 1937	Brunete
Drury-Fuller	George Norman	Maidenhead	September 1938	Sierra Caballs
Duffy	James	Glasgow	April 1938	Aragon
Dunbar	Arthur Edward	London	July 1937	Brunete
Duncan	Richard Hamilton	Tillicoultry	September 1938	Flix
Duncombe	Thomas	London	3 April 1938	Gandesa
Durkin	Martin	Middlesbrough	March1938	Aragon
Durston	William Francis	Wembley	September 1938	Sierra Caballs
Edelman	Sidney	London	April 1938	Aragon
Elias	Phillip	Leeds	13 February 1937	Executed whilst a prisoner at Jarama
Elliott	Robert S	Northumberland	July 1937	Villanueva de la Cañada
Elliott	Thomas	Worthing	June 1937	Jarama
Epstein	Samuel	Johannesburg	April 1938	Aragon
Esteban	Victoriano	Swansea	July 1937	Brunete
Evans	Edwin Arnold	Glasgow	20 March 1938	In Tarragona hospital from wounds sustained at Caspe
Fairchild	John E	London	March 1938	Aragon
Featherstone	William Henry	London	November 1938	Vich hospital
Felton	Fred	Rochester	February 1937	Jarama
Ferguson	John	Glasgow/Canada	April 1938	Aragon
Fink	Sydney Samson	Salford	10-17 March 1938	Belchite
Finnan	Andrew	Dundee	March 1938	Belchite
Fisher	Herbert Douglas	Romsey	November 1938	In Vich hospital from wounds sustained in July on the Ebro
Flecks	Thomas	Blantyre	April 1937	Chimorra
Flynn	Thomas F	Glasgow	April 1937	Chimorra
Foley	James	London/Dublin	December 1936	Lopera
Fox	Anthony	Dublin	28 December 1936	Lopera
Fox	Ralph	London	28 December 1936	Lopera
Fox	William H	Blantyre	15 April 1937	Jarama
Foxall	Charles Leslie	Sale	12 February 1937	Jarama
Francis	Archibald Frank	Reading	9 March 1938	Belchite

Francis	Silvio	London	January 1938	Teruel
Freedman	Frederick	London	January 1938	Teruel
Fretwell	George Ernest	Penygroes	February 1937	Jarama
Frillingham	Joseph	Bury	20 January 1938	Teruel
Fry	Harold	Edinburgh	13 October 1937	Fuentes de Ebro
Gallagher	Michael	Wigan	July 1937	Brunete
Garland	Peter	Glasgow	30 January 1938	Teruel
Gaunt	Thomas	Chesterfield	March 1938	Aragon
Gauntlett	William	Glasgow	July 1938	Hill 666, Gandesa
Gaydon	Ronald	Bristol	February 1937	Jarama
Gibbons	Thomas	London	July 1937	Brunete
Giles	William J	Liverpool	13 February 1937	Jarama
Gilmour	John	Prestonpans	12 February 1937	Jarama
Glacken	Patrick	Greenock	21 January 1938	Teruel
Glaser	Benjamin	London	11 September 1938	Sierra Pandols
Glasson	Patrick Harry	Redruth	July 1937	Brunete
Glen	Robert	Alexandria	September 1938	Sierra Pandols
Gold	Alfred	London	27 February 1937	Jarama
Gomm	Harry	London	27 February 1937	Jarama
Goodfellow	Charles	Bellshill	July 1937	Brunete
Goodison	Michael	Salford	April 1938	Aragon
Goodman	Robert W	Nottingham	12 February 1937	Jarama
Gorman	George F	Folkestone	22 September 1938	Sierra Caballs
Gough	William Joseph	Luton, Beds	20 December 1936	Boadilla
Grant	Robert Alexander	London	March 1938	Calaceite
Grant	Terry James	Nottingham	March 1938	Aragon
Green	George Frederick	Stockport	23 September 1938	Sierra Caballs
Green	Leo James	Dublin	February 1937	Jarama
Green	Maurice	Manchester	March 1938	Aragon
Greenwood	James	Ashton-under-Lyne	1937	Unknown
Grierson	Robert	Dumfries	March 1938	Aragon
Gross	Harry	London	July 1937	Brunete
Grossart	David	Glasgow	April 1937	In hospital from wounds sustained at Jarama
Guerin	Edward	London	25 August 1937	Quinto
Guest	David Haden	London	July 1938	Gandesa
Gura	Mark	London	February 1937	Jarama
Hall	Alexander	Plymouth	August 1938	Sierra Pandols
Hall	John	Glasgow	March 1938	Belchite
Halloran	David	Middlesbrough	27 February 1937	Jarama
Hamill	Thomas	Glasgow	February 1937	Jarama
Hamm	Sidney	Cardiff	July 1937	Villanueva de la Cañada
Harding	James Myles M	Stockton-on-Tees	September 1938	Sierra Caballs
Hardy	George	London	April 1938	Calaceite
Harkins	Joseph	Clydebank	30 July 1938	Hill 481, Gandesa
Harris	Augustus	Liverpool	July 1937	Brunete
Harris	T Jack	Llanelly	2 April 1937	Jarama
Harvey	Alex G	Glasgow	13 February 1937	Jarama
Hempel	Martin	London	July 1938	Gandesa
Henderson	David	Glasgow	February 1937	Jarama
Henderson	James	London	July 1937	Brunete
Henderson	Richard	Kirkcaldy	April 1938	Aragon
Henry	William	Belfast	23 February 1937	Jarama
Hickman	Ivor Rae	Petersfield	22-23 September 1938	Sierra Caballs

Hilliard	Robert Martin	Letchworth	18 February 1937	In Benicasim hospital from wounds sustained at Jarama
Hillock	Andrew	Kirkcaldy	July 1937	In UK from typhus contracted in Spain
Hoare	Arnold	Leeds	March 1938	Aragon
Hobbs	Albert George	Chelmsford	September 1938	Sierra Caballs
Hollanby	George Arthur	London	April 1938	Gandesa
Hone	Roger Basil Bentoit	London	August 1938	Ebro
Horradge	David	Huddersfield	July 1937	Brunete
Howarth	John	Manchester	March 1938	Aragon
Hunt	Vincent John	London	10 July 1937	Brunete
Hunter	William Dykes	Glasgow	March 1938	Aragon
Huson	Leslie	Bristol	May 1938	In hospital of pneumonia
Hyman	Charles	Glasgow	30 March 1937	In hospital from wounds sustained at Jarama
Hyndman	James	Glasgow	12 January 1937	Las Rozas
Jackman	Edward F	Liverpool	February 1937	Jarama
Jackson	George	Cowdenbeath	19 August 1938	Sierra Pandols
Jackson	William	Oldham	April 1938	Gandesa
James	Sidney George	Treherbert	18 September 1938	Sierra Pandols
Jasper	WE	London	13 February 1937	Jarama
Jeans	Arnold	Manchester	December 1936	Boadilla
Jobling	Wilf	Blaydon-on-Tyne	27 February 1937	Jarama
Johnson	Thomas	London	March 1938	Belchite
Jones	DE	London	July 1938	Ebro
Jones	David Joseph	Penygraig	13 February 1937	Jarama
Jones	H Fred	London	11 November 1936	Casa de Campo
Jones	James J	London/Dublin	July 1938	Ebro
Jones	Thomas Howell	Aberdare	25 August 1938	Sierra Pandols
Jordan	Leonard	Manchester	July 1937	Brunete
Jordan	Ronald Percy	Wembley	March 1938	Caspe
Julius	Emanuel	London	18 October 1936	Alcubierre
Kamenos	Anthony	Greece	April 1937	In hospital from wounds sustained at Jarama
Katsaronas	Panayiotis	London/Cyprus	13 February 1937	Jarama
Keegan	William	Glasgow	July 1937	Villanueva de la Cañada
Keery	Frank	Durham	July 1938	Gandesa
Kelly	George	Greenock	July 1938	Hill 481, Gandesa
Kelly	Joseph M	Dublin	July 1937	Brunete
Kelly	Michael J	Ballinsloe	7 July 1937	Brunete
Kelter	William	Glasgow	March 1938	Gandesa
Kemp	Allan	Port Glasgow	January 1938	Teruel
Kenny	WR	Manchester	1937	From wounds sustained at Jarama
Kent	Jack	New Zealand	31 May 1937	Drowned on SS City of Barcelona
Keogh	James H	Ashton	17 March 1938	Calaceite
Kermode	James S	Airdrie	12 January 1937	Las Rozas
Kerr	Thomas A	Belfast	9 October 1938	Of typhoid in Vich hospital
Kerry	Edward	London	July 1937	Brunete
Killick	T Fred	Southport	12 February 1937	Jarama
Kirk	Robert	Liverpool	February 1937	Jarama

Knottman	James	Manchester	12 January 1937	Las Rozas
Knowles	William	London	February 1937	Jarama
Lacey	Clifford F	London	September 1938	Sierra Caballs
Lamb	George Cresswell	London	April 1938	Gandesa
Langmead	William H	London	July 1937	Brunete
Large	Lionel George	Enfield	April 1938	Of exposure as a prisoner
Larlham	C Anthony	London	October 1937	Fuentes de Ebro
Laughlin	William P	Belfast	6 July 1937	Villanueva de la Cañada
Laughran	James	Motherwell	July 1937	Brunete
Lawrie	John	Twickenham	August 1938	Gandesa
Laws	Harold Charles	Southampton	February 1938	Segura de los Baños
Lawther	Clifford	Hexham	12 February 1937	Jarama
Lee	Samuel Ralph	London	27 February 1937	Jarama
Lees	Joseph Maynard	Oldham	July 1937	Brunete
Leppard	Alexander	London	23 February 1937	Jarama
Leslie	George S	Kingston upon Thames	July 1937	Brunete
Levin	Ariel	London	March 1938	Aragon
Lewis	Sidney	London	July 1938	Gandesa
Lichfield	Alfred	Gateshead	July 1938	Gandesa
Livesay	Michael EJ	London	June 1937	Segovia
Loader	Thomas Charles	London	December 1937	Of a fever in Vich hospital
Lobban	John	Alexandria	September 1938	Sierra Caballs
Lomax	RK	Shrewsbury	17 February 1937	Jarama
Lower	William Ernest	Sunderland	31 May 1937	Drowned on SS City of Barcelona
Lyons	James	Glasgow	February 1937	Jarama
Mackie	Robert H	Sunderland	July 1937	Brunete
Mackie	William	London	March 1938	Aragon
MacLaurin	Griffin Campbell	Cambridge	9 November 1936	Casa de Campo
Madero	Alexander	Louth	April 1938	In Figueras hospital from wounds
Mandell	Montague	London/Manchester	12 February 1937	Jarama
Marks	Alfred J	London	July 1937	Brunete
Marshall	James Spy	Clydebank	March 1938	Aragon
Maskey	Bert	Manchester	14 February 1937	Jarama
Mason	Norman	Barnsley	March 1938	Aragon
Mason	Robert	Edinburgh	27 February 1937	Jarama
Masters	Sam Maurice	London	July 1937	Brunete
Matthews	Herbert	Cuffley	April 1938	Gandesa
Maugham	Leslie Charles	Kettering	January 1938	Teruel
May	Christopher	Wallasey	August 1937	Aragon
May	Michael	Dublin	28 December 1936	Lopera
McCabe	Albert	Liverpool	25 August 1937	Brunete
McCabe	Frank	Dundee	August 1937	Quinto
McCafferty	Bernard	Banffshire	March 1938	Aragon
McCulloch	Frederick	Glasgow	30 October 1937	Fuentes de Ebro
McDade	Alex	Glasgow	6 July 1937	Brunete
McDonald	Donald	Brighton	April 1938	Gandesa
McDonald	Robert	Glasgow	31 May 1937	Drowned on SS City of Barcelona
McElroy	James	Wishaw	May 1937	Jarama
McGrath	Henry	Belfast	September 1938	Sierra Caballs
McGregor	Alexander	London	19 January 1938	Teruel

Antifascistas

McGregor	William Scott	Dublin	23 September 1938	Sierra Caballs
McGrotty	Eamon	Dublin	27 February 1937	Jarama
McGuire	William	Dundee	28 February 1937	Jarama
McHugh	James	Dundee	March 1938	Gandesa
McKay	David	Glasgow	April 1938	Gandesa
McKenzie	David	Glasgow	March 1938	Aragon
McKeown	Andrew	Glasgow	July 1937	Brunete
McKeown	George	Liverpool	12 February 1937	Jarama
McKissock	James	Glasgow	April 1937	In an accident at Alcalá de Henares
McLanders	John	Dundee	April 1937	Jarama
McLaughlin	William	Belfast	July 1937	Brunete
McLennagan	John	Greenock	September 1938	In hospital in Tarragona
McLeod	Charles Daniel	Aberdeen	19 August 1938	Sierra Pandols
McLeod	Thomas Scott	Liverpool	March 1938	Aragon
McMorrow	James	Glasgow	10-17 March 1938	Aragon
McMullan	William	Bellshill	20 January 1937	Teruel
McNally	Arthur John	Birmingham	March 1938	Aragon
McWhirter	Thomas F	Glasgow	March 1938	Caspe
Meehan	John	Galway	28 December 1936	Lopera
Mellors	John	Nottingham	March 1938	Caspe
Mennell	Cecil Frederick	London	January 1938	Teruel
Meredith	William G	Glasgow	6 July 1937	Villanueva de la Cañada
Messer	Martin J	Glasgow	December 1936	Boadilla
Miller	John	Glasgow	March 1938	Aragon
Miller	Maurice Lionel	Hull	August 1938	Hill 666, Gandesa
Moir	James S	Perth	July 1937	Brunete
Moore	James Arthur	Portsmouth	January 1939	Mortally wounded at Sierra Pandols
Moore	Thomas P	Manchester	20 January 1938	Teruel
Morcom	William Arthur	Australia	September 1938	Gandesa
Morrice	Kenneth Edward	Aberdeen	2 August 1938	Gandesa
Morris	Arthur Wigley	Canada	27 February 1937	Jarama
Morris	Philip	London	12 February 1937	Jarama
Morris	Samuel	Ammanford	July 1937	Brunete
Morris	William	Llanelly	July 1937	Brunete
Mortakis	Christos C	Cyprus	April 1938	Gandesa
Moss	Richard Arthur	London	April 1938	Gandesa
Mudie	John D	Dundee	March 1938	Caspe
Muir	Alexander	London	3 February 1937	Jarama
Murphy	Daniel	Cardiff	April 1938	Gandesa
Murphy	Jame	Glasgow	March 1938	Caspe
Murphy	Peter	London	July 1937	Brunete
Murray	Benjamin	Belfast	March 1938	Aragon
Murray	James	Dundee	March 1938	Caspe
Murray	James	Glasgow	July 1937	Brunete
Murray	William	Glasgow	July 1937	Brunete
Nalty	Jack	Dublin	23 September 1938	Sierra Caballs
Nash	Max	London	July 1938	Gandesa
Nathan	George Montague	London	26 July 1937	Brunete
Neary	Frank	USA	February 1937	Jarama
Ness	John Bruce	Dundee	July 1938	Gandesa
Newbury	Fred	Manchester	20 February 1937	Jarama
Newman	Peter John	Liverpool	27 February 1937	Jarama

Newsome	Arthur	Sheffield	27 December 1937	Lopera
Nicholaou	Demidrus	London/Cyprus	March 1938	Gandesa
Nolan	Michael	Dublin	28 December 1936	Lopera
Norbury	James Thomas	Liverpool	February 1937	Jarama
Norton	Frank Joseph	Liverpool	27 February 1937	Jarama
Nuns	Michael	London	March 1938	Aragon
O'Brien	Frank Duffy	London	14 or 16 February 1938	Teruel
O'Brien	Thomas T	Liverpool	27 February 1937	Jarama
O'Day	Peter	London	17 March 1938	Belchite or Caspe
Oldershaw	Thomas	London	16 March 1938	Aragon
O'Neill	Richard	Belfast	14 February 1937	Jarama
O'Nichen	Leonard	Stoke	March 1938	Aragon
Ormsby	Ruth Hannah Rutledge	Co. Sligo	May 1938	Barcelona
Orphanides	Loukas	Cyprus	March 1938	Belchite
O'Sullivan	Patrick	Dublin	July 1938	Gandesa
Overton	Bert	Stockton-on-Tees	July 1937	Brunete
Owen	Frank	Mardy	July 1937	Brunete
Owens	John David	Liverpool	February 1937	Jarama
Palmer	George William	London	12 January 1937	Las Rozas
Palzeard	John G	South Shields	February 1937	Jarama
Park	Alexander	Glasgow	12 March 1938	Aragon
Parkes	Albert	Manchester	July 1937	Brunete
Patten	Tom	Co. Mayo	December 1936	Boadilla
Paul	Edward Robert	London	February 1937	Jarama
Pearson	Henry CH	London	July 1938	In hospital from wounds sustained at the Ebro
Perdicos	Nikos	Cyprus	14 February 1937	Jarama
Perry	Leonard	Enfield	April 1938	Gandesa
Perryman	Arthur James	London	9 April 1938	In Saragossa hospital as a prisoner
Perzoff	Marc	Russia/Geneva	March 1937	Jarama
Peterson	John	Liverpool	April 1938	Gandesa
Petrie	Edward William	London	July 1937	Villanueva de la Cañada
Picton	Thomas Isaac	Treherbert	April 1938	Executed whilst a prisoner at Bilbao
Pitman	Joseph	London	April 1937	Chimorra
Plumb	Frederick Arthur	Luton	13 February 1937	Jarama
Porter	Arthur	Manchester	12 February 1937	Jarama
Procter	Frank John	Liverpool	August 1938	Sierra Pandols
Pryme	Lawrence G	London	August 1938	In Vallcarca hospital from wounds sustained at Hill 481, Gandesa
Purves	Alexander	London	April 1938	Gandesa
Quinlan	Frank	London	June 1937	Drowned, Mondejar
Quinlan	Maurice P	Waterford	February 1937	Jarama
Rabone	Albert Edward	Gosport	Spring 1938	Killed in an accident on board a ship in Barcelona
Rae	James	Glasgow	February 1937	Jarama
Rawson	Harry R	Oldham	27 December 1936	Lopera
Rebbechi	Kevin	Melbourne	January 1939	In Vich hospital of typhus
Redmond	John Sean	Liverpool	March 1938	Aragon
Reynolds	Harry	Newcastle	February 1937	Jarama
Rickman	John Pascal	Sherborne	17 April 1937	Jarama

Riddell	John	Glasgow	September 1937	In Murcia hospital from wounds sustained at Brunete
Riley	John Jack	Glasgow	19 January 1938	Teruel
Riordan	John Edward	London	April 1938	Aragon
Roach	Joseph Cless	Leeds	March 1938	Gandesa
Robertson	Frederick H	Rainham, Kent	15 February 1937	Jarama
Robilliard	Victor	Dagenham	October 1938	In Mataro hospital
Robinson	Arthur Leonard	Hartlepool	13 October 1937	Fuentes de Ebro
Rodgers	Frank William Sefton	Unknown	5 March 1937	In Villarejo hospital
Rodriguez	Roman R	Dowlais	July 1937	Brunete
Ross	John McLeod	Edinburgh	17 March 1938	Belchite or Caspe, Aragon
Rossides	Sergios	Cyprus	April 1938	Gandesa
Rowney	William C	London	13 February 1937	Jarama
Rutherford	James	Edinburgh	April 1938	Executed whilst a prisoner at Burgos
Ryan	Maurice Emmett	Bedfordshire	5 August 1938	Gandesa
Ryder	Edward	London	June 1938	Shot at Palencia whilst a prisoner
Samson	David	Dundee	July 1937	Brunete
Scott	Cyril James	London	August 1938	Died in El Perelló hospital from wounds sustained at the Ebro in July
Scott	Humphrey Gilbert	Moscow	21 April 1937	Chimorra
Scott	James	Swansea	March 1938	Caspe
Scott	John	Lincoln	23 February 1937	Jarama
Seal	William 'Joe'	London	February 1937	Jarama
Segal	Nathan	London	27 December 1936	Lopera
Shammah	Victor	Manchester	March 1938	Aragon
Sheehan	Don T	Brighton	March 1938	Aragon
Sherpenzeel	Jacobus Johannes	Rotterdam	July 1938	Gandesa
Shields	Bernard	Glasgow	March 1938	Caspe
Shields	Joseph	Glasgow	February 1937	Jarama
Shields	Robert	Glasgow	September 1938	Sierra Caballs
Silcock	Thomas	Liverpool	13 February 1937	Jarama
Sim	Ernest	Aberdeen	September 1938	Sierra Caballs
Simmons	Charles James	Portsmouth	27 February 1937	Jarama
Skinner	Alwynne W	Neath	1938	Ebro
Smillie	Robert Ramsay	Larkhall	12 June 1937	Of appendicitis in Mataro jail, Valencia
Smith	Albert Clement	Manchester	August 1938	Executed whilst a prisoner
Smith	David	Glasgow	February 1937	Jarama
Smith	Harold J	Gateshead	February 1937	Jarama
Smith	John	Irvine	September 1938	Sierra Caballs
Smith	Malcolm	Dundee	19 August 1938	Hill 666, Sierra Pandols
Smith	William	Birkenhead	March 1938	Aragon
Sollenberger	Randall	New York	26 July 1937	Brunete
Spencer	Frederick	Pontefract	12 February 1937	Jarama
Sprigg	Christopher St John	London	12 February 1937	Jarama
Sproston	Walter	Manchester	March 1938	Calaceite
Stalker	Albert Kenneth	London	12 February 1937	Jarama
Steele	John	Falkirk	May 1937	In air-raid at Albacete
Steigman	Nathan	London	27 February 1937	Jarama

Stephens	Terence Edward	Bristol	July 1938	In hospital in Barcelona from blood poisoning
Stevens	John	London	13 February 1937	Executed whilst a prisoner at Jarama
Stevens	John Ernest	Melbourne	July 1937	Brunete
Stevenson	Joseph	Bellshill	February 1938	Of typhoid in hospital
Stewart	James W	Wallasey	February 1937	Jarama
Stickland	Leslie R	London	February 1937	Jarama
Stockdale	George Edward	Leeds	25 July 1938	Gandesa
Stott	Maurice	Rochdale	12 February 1937	Jarama
Straney	James	Belfast	July 1938	Gandesa
Strangward	Harold James R	Neath	August 1938	Hill 481, Gandesa
Sullivan	James	Glasgow	July 1938	Gandesa
Swindells	Edward Maurice	Manchester	February 1937	Jarama
Sykes	Frederick	Sheffield	February 1937	Jarama
Sylvester	John	London	February 1937	Jarama
Symes	Robert A	London	9 November 1936	Casa de Campo
Tadden	William John	Dundee	27 February 1937	Jarama
Tagg	Herbert	Doncaster	27 February 1937	Jarama
Tallis	Walter	London	April 1938	Gandesa
Tankelovitch	Louis	London	March 1938	Belchite
Tapsell	Walter	London	1 April 1938	Calaceite
Tattam	Edward	Sunderland	March 1938	Aragon
Tattam	William E	Sunderland	17 July 1937	Brunete
Taylor	Gilbert	Cardiff	April 1938	Calaceite
Taylor	Jack Donald	London	12 February 1937	Jarama
Thomas	Brazell	Llanelly	30 July 1938	Gandesa
Thomas	Fred JGC	Gillingham	12 February 1937	Jarama
Thompson	Andrew	Great Lumley	19 January 1938	Teruel
Tinga	A	Netherlands	February 1937	Jarama
Traill	Robert	Radyr	July 1937	Villanueva de la Cañada
Trauber	Abraham	London	22 September 1938	Sierra Caballs
Tumilson	William James	Belfast	14 March 1937	Jarama
Turnhill	George Ernest	Worksop	January 1938	Teruel
Unthank	John	Middlesbrough	April 1937	In Benicasim hospital from wounds sustained at Jarama
Verstage	Halcrow A	London	24 February 1937	Chinchón
Walsh	David	Ballina	19 January 1938	Teruel
Walsh	James Erskine	Liverpool	12 February 1937	Jarama
Walsh	Samuel Edward	Newcastle	July 1937	Brunete
Warbrick	Frederick	Teddington	March 1938	Caspe
Ward	Robert	Manchester	14 June 1937	In Colmenar hospital from wounds sustained at Jarama
Wardle	Robert William	Hull	31 March 1938	Calaceite
Wark	James	Airdrie	February 1937	Jarama
Watson	Jack F	Worcester	27 February 1937	Jarama
Watson	William	Glasgow	July 1938	Gandesa
Watt	James R	Swansea	August 1938	Gandesa
Watts	Roy Theodore	Leicester	September 1938	Sierra Caballs
Webb	William Albert	London	25 February 1937	Jarama
Westfield	George	Liverpool	10 October 1937	Fuentes de Ebro
Whalley	Eric	Mansfield	October 1937	Fuentes de Ebro

Whalley	John	London	March 1938	Aragon
Wheeler	James	London	18 February 1937	Jarama
White	Frederick J	Ogmore Vale	6 July 1937	Villanueva de la Cañada
White	James S	London	13 February 1937	Jarama
Whitehead	Frank	Manchester	24 February 1937	Jarama
Wilkinson	Edgar F	Sunderland	February 1937	Jarama
Wilkinson	Norman	Manchester	February 1937	Jarama
Williams	John E	Ammanford	July 1937	Brunete
Williams	Percival E	Swindon	March 1938	Caspe
Willoughby	William	Vancouver	March 1938	Aragon
Winfield	Bernard George	Nottingham	19 January 1938	Teruel
Winter	Andrew	Glasgow	July 1937	Brunete
Wise	Harold	London	12 January 1937	In hospital in Madrid from wounds sustained at Las Rozas
Wolstencroft	Clifford	Oldham	10 March 1938	Belchite
Woodhouse	Alfred	Mansfield	July 1937	Brunete
Woods	Thomas	Dublin	December 1936	Córdoba
Yates	Anthony	Glasgow	February 1937	Jarama
Yates	Stephen	London	9 November 1936	Casa de Campo
Young	William John	Sydney	July 1938	Gandesa
Zamorra	Frank	Abercrave	18 or 19 January 1938	Teruel

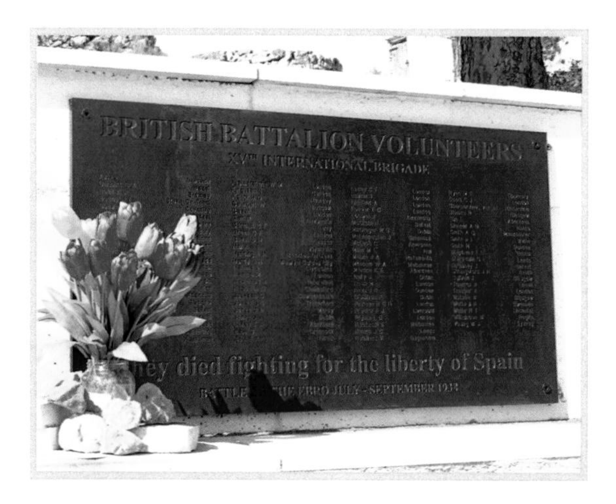

Memorials in Spain to fallen International Brigaders; above: a plaque dedicated to four British writers and Irish poet Charles Donnelly at the Residencia de Estudiantes arts centre in Madrid; left: the names of 90 members of the British Battalion who were killed in the Battle of the Ebro on a memorial plaque at Pinell de Bray, near Gandesa.

Suggested Further Reading

For a full bibliography, visit the IBMT's website:
www.international-brigades.org.uk/british_volunteers

The Spanish Civil War

Graham, Helen. The Spanish Civil War: A Very Short Introduction. Oxford: Oxford University Press, 2005.

Howson, Gerald. Arms for Spain: The Untold Story of the Spanish Civil War. London: John Murray, 1998.

Preston, Paul. A Concise History of the Spanish Civil War. London: Fontana, 1996.

Thomas, Hugh. The Spanish Civil War. 4th edition, London: Penguin, 2003.

British volunteers in the International Brigades

Alexander, Bill. British Volunteers for Liberty. London: Lawrence & Wishart, 1982.

Baxell, Richard. British Volunteers in the Spanish Civil War: The British Battalion in the International Brigades. 1936-1939. London: Routledge/Cañada Blanch Studies on Contemporary Spain, 2004 and Pontypool: Warren & Pell, 2006.

Gray, Daniel. Homage to Caledonia. Scotland and the Spanish Civil War. Edinburgh: Luath Press, 2008.

Hopkins, James K. Into the Heart of the Fire: The British in the Spanish Civil War. Palo Alto: Stanford University Press, 1998.

Marx Memorial Library, London, home of the International Brigade Memorial Archive.

Selected British volunteers' memoirs

Doyle, Bob. Brigadista. An Irishman's Fight Against Fascism. Blackrock: Currach Press, 2006.

Greening, Edwin. From Aberdare to Albacete. Pontypool: Warren & Pell, 2006.

Gregory, Walter. The Shallow Grave: A Memoir of the Spanish Civil War. London: Victor Gollancz, 1986.

Orwell, George. Homage to Catalonia. London: Secker & Warburg, 1938.

Thomas, Fred. To Tilt at Windmills: A Memoir of the Spanish Civil War. East Lansing: State University of Michigan Press, 1996.

Wheeler, George, edited by David Leach. To Make the People Smile Again. Newcastle: Zymurgy, 2003.

Williams, Alun Menai. From the Rhondda to the Ebro. Pontypool: Warren & Pell, 2004.

Collections of memoirs

Arthur, Max. The Real Band of Brothers: First-hand Accounts from the Last British Survivors of the Spanish Civil War. London: Collins, 2009.

Darman, Peter. Heroic Voices of the Spanish Civil War: Memories from the International Brigades. London: New Holland, 2009.

Fyrth, Jim and Sally Alexander. Women's Voices from the Spanish Civil War. London: Lawrence & Wishart, 2008.

MacDougall, Ian, ed. Voices from the Spanish Civil War: Personal Recollections of Scottish Volunteers in Republican Spain, 1936-1939. Edinburgh: Polygon, 1986.

Aid Spain and the medical volunteers

Buchanan, Tom. Britain and the Spanish Civil War. Cambridge: Cambridge University Press, 1997.

Fyrth, Jim. The Signal Was Spain. London: Lawrence & Wishart, 1986.

Jackson, Angela. British Women and the Spanish Civil War, 1936-39. London: Routledge, 2002 and Barcelona: Warren & Pell, 2009.

Art for the cause

Cunningham, Valentine, ed. The Penguin Book of Spanish Civil War Verse. Harmondsworth: Penguin, 1980.

Jump, Jim, ed. Poems from Spain: British and Irish International Brigaders on the Spanish Civil War. London: Lawrence & Wishart, 2006.

Morris, Lynda and Robert Radford. The Story of the Artists International Association 1933-1953. Oxford: Museum of Modern Art, 1983.

The anti-fascist fight continues

Alexander, Bill. Say No to Franco: The Struggle Never Stopped 1939-1975. London: Lawrence & Wishart, 1992.

Jones, Jack. Union Man. London: Collins, 1986 and Pontypool: Warren & Pell, 2008.

Preston, Paul. Franco. A Biography. London: Fontana, 1993.

Remembering the International Brigades

Buchanan, Tom. The Impact of the Spanish Civil War on Britain: War, Loss and Memory. Eastbourne: Sussex University Press, 2007.

Toynbee, Philip, ed. The Distant Drum: Reflections on the Spanish Civil War. London: Sidgwick & Jackson, 1976.

Williams, Colin, Bill Alexander and John Gorman. Memorials of the Spanish Civil War. Stroud: Sutton, 1996.